Fujifilm X-H2 User Reference

A Comprehensive Companion for Mastering the
Features and Functions of the X-H2 Camera

By

Clyde Bertram

Table of Content

INTRODUCTION

The Fujifilm X-H2 is a powerful and versatile mirrorless camera that is perfect for photographers of all levels. Whether you're a seasoned pro or just starting out, the X-H2 has the features and capabilities to help you capture stunning images and videos.

The X-H2 marks a watershed moment in Fujifilm's X-series lineup. It's a culmination of cutting-edge technology, meticulous design, and unwavering dedication to the photographer's craft. Within its magnesium alloy shell lies a powerhouse sensor paired with the lightning-fast X-Processor 5, ready to capture moments with breathtaking clarity and speed.

But a camera is more than just its specs. It's an extension of your artistic eye, a tool to translate fleeting emotions into timeless images. This guide is your trusted companion on that journey. We'll navigate the intricacies of the X-H2's controls, delve into its shooting modes and menus, and unlock the secrets of its advanced features.

In this user guide, we'll take you through everything you need to know about your new camera. We'll start with the basics, such as how to set up your camera and take your first photos. Then, we'll move on to more advanced topics, such as how to use the different shooting modes, adjust the exposure settings, and capture creative effects.

By the end of this guide, you'll be well on your way to mastering the X-H2 and taking your photography to the next level.

CHAPTER 1: GETTING THE CAMERA UP AND RUNNING

Preparing the Camera for Initial Use

Shoulder Strap

If you're anything like me, you might be tempted to skip this part because who needs instructions for putting on a camera strap? Well, I've been doing it wrong for 30 years. My way left the straps hanging and the ends poking my arms. Don't make a mistake – check out the diagrams below to correctly attach the shoulder strap. (Before you start, look at the camera manual for installing strap clips if they're not already on.)

1. Put the strap through the small plastic piece and the camera strap hole.

2. Pass the strap back through the plastic piece, then through the farthest hole in the bigger stopper.

3. Bring the strap up through the closest hole in the big stopper.

4. Tighten the straps and repeat to attach the other end to the opposite camera strap hole.

The Battery

Your camera comes with a rechargeable battery called NP-W235. If you ever need a new battery, buy a real Fujifilm one. Other brands might not be safe and could cause a fire or explosion. Now, let's talk about putting the battery into the camera.

Inserting the Battery

1. Turn off the camera.

2. Open the battery compartment by sliding the latch and flipping the cover.

3. Put the battery into the camera with the side of the contact first, using it to press the latch. If it's tough, check the battery's orientation.

4. Close the cover and slide the latch back to lock it.

Removing the Battery

1. Turn off the camera.

2. Open the battery compartment by sliding the latch towards the lens side and flipping it open.

3. Push the battery latch to release the battery.

4. Close the battery compartment and slide the latch back to lock it.

Battery Charging

Put the battery in the camera, and use the USB cable and AC adapter to charge it. Connect the plug adapter to the AC adapter, then plug the USB cable into the camera. Finally, plug the AC adapter into a power outlet indoors. It will take around 180 minutes to charge. Alternatively, you can use a computer with a powered USB connection, but it will take about 600 minutes, and make sure the charging input is 5 V/500 mA.

The light on the camera shows the battery status:

- If the light is on, the battery is charging.

- If the light is off, the battery is fully charged.

- If the light is blinking, there's a battery error.

You can buy the BC-W235 battery charger to charge two batteries externally.

Memory Cards

Memory cards are essential for photos and videos. The Fujifilm X-H2 can use CFexpress cards in Slot 1 and SD cards in Slot 2. You can use a card in each slot, but you don't have to.

Inserting the Memory Card

1. Turn off the camera.

2. Open the cover for the memory card slot.

3. Put the memory card in, ensuring the label faces the back of the camera. Push it down until it clicks. The top slot is Slot 1, and the bottom is Slot 2.

4. Close the cover and latch it.

Removing the Memory Card

1. Turn off the camera and check that the light is not on.

2. Open the cover for the memory card slot.

3. Carefully insert the memory card into the camera, then take it out.

4. Close and latch the memory card slot cover again.

Shooting Without a Card

You can take pictures on the camera without a memory card, but those pictures won't be saved. To avoid any hassle, consider turning off this feature in case you forget to insert a memory card before taking photos. This option exists so that when cameras are on display in stores, people can try out the camera without needing a memory card.

Configuring Shooting Without a Card

1. Go to MENU, click the Setting icon, choose [BUTTON/DIAL SETTING], and select [SHOOT WITHOUT CARD].

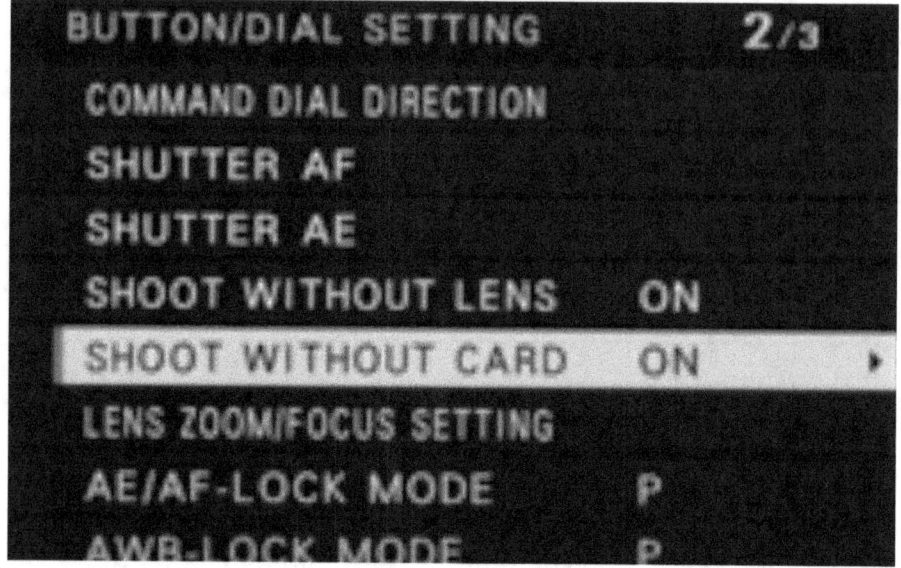

2. Choose:

- **[ON]:** Lets you take a picture even without a memory card.

- **[OFF]:** Prevents the camera from taking a picture without a memory card.

Lens

Lenses are super important for your camera. Even if your camera is fancy, your pictures will only be great if the lens is good. Lenses often last longer than your camera, so it's smart to understand them and the jargon. You can even try renting lenses online or at a local photography shop.

Lens Compatibility

When picking a lens, start by figuring out the mount your camera has. Fujifilm has two main types for their X series cameras: G-mount for GFX-Series cameras and X-mount for APS-C sensor cameras like the X-H2.

You can use lenses from other brands like Meike on your Fujifilm camera, but you might need some features, like adjusting the aperture in the camera. Instead, you may manually change the aperture using the lens's ring.

Focal length

The focal length, shown in lens descriptions with "mm" numbers, is crucial for photographers. It tells you how much the lens magnifies and affects the field of view. A bigger focal length means more magnification and a larger subject in your photos.

Crop Factor

The X-H2 has a smaller APS-C sensor than the usual full-frame 35mm sensor.

Because of this smaller sensor, the X-H2 has a 1.5x crop factor. So, if you use an 18mm lens, it's like using a 27mm lens on a full frame 35mm sensor camera. This is calculated by multiplying the lens focal length (18) by the crop factor (1.5), resulting in approximately 27. When a lens is described, you might see "35mm equivalent" with another focal length, showing the lens's view compared to a full-frame sensor camera.

Focal Length Classification

Lenses come in three types: wide-angle, standard, and telephoto. It's good to have one of each for your collection.

Wide Angle Lens

A lens is called a wide angle if it has a focal length below 35mm. These lenses are suitable for capturing big views like landscapes. They can get everything from close to far away, which is helpful for tight spaces or inside shots where you can't step back much. Wide-angle lenses also make more things look sharp in the photo.

Standard Lens

Regular lenses have a focal range of around 50mm (35-70mm). A 50mm lens on a full-frame camera is like seeing through the human eye. People often use regular lenses for street or documentary-style photos.

Telephoto Lens

Lenses with focal lengths longer than around 70mm are called telephoto lenses. These lenses make faraway things look closer, making them great for taking pictures of animals or sports from a distance. The longer telephoto lenses also create a blurry background effect.

Focal Length and Perspective

If you use different camera zooms, even if your main subject stays the same size, the way things look in the background changes. If you zoom out, you capture more of the background, making it seem wider. On the other hand, zooming in makes the background look narrower and closer to the main subject. The more you zoom in, the flatter the scene looks, and things seem closer together, even if they're far apart.

Next, lenses can make things close to the camera look much bigger, and things far away look smaller. Shorter focal length lenses exaggerate this effect, making close subjects appear larger and distant subjects smaller.

Zoom vs Prime

Prime lenses have a fixed focal length, like the Fujinon XF 14mm F2.8 R lens, while zoom lenses, such as the XF16-80mm F4 R OIS WR lens, let you adjust the focal length within a set range (e.g., 16mm to 80mm).

People might pick prime lenses because they're often more affordable, lighter, and have wider maximum apertures, even though zoom lenses provide more flexibility.

How to Attach a Lens

1. Turn left to remove the lens cover from the back of the lens and the front of the camera.

2. Match the marks on the camera and lens.

3. Insert the lens into the camera and turn it right until it clicks.

How to Detach a Lens

1. Turn the camera towards you, press the lens release button, and twist the lens counterclockwise until it stops. This is the lens detach button.

2. Pull the lens away from the camera, then quickly put the body cap on the camera or switch to another lens. Don't forget to put the lens caps back on both ends of the removed lens.

How to Use the Lens

Your camera lens might have three adjustable rings—aperture, focus, and zoom. Some lenses lack an aperture ring, and the camera controls it instead. Prime lenses, which don't zoom, won't have a zoom ring. There might also be switches on the lens, which we'll discuss in their respective sections.

Shooting Without a Lens Attached

You can take pictures without a lens using the camera. If the lens isn't designed for the Fujifilm X-H2, the camera might not recognize it, so you'd need to set it to shoot without a lens. It can be useful, for example, when connecting your camera to a telescope for astrophotography.

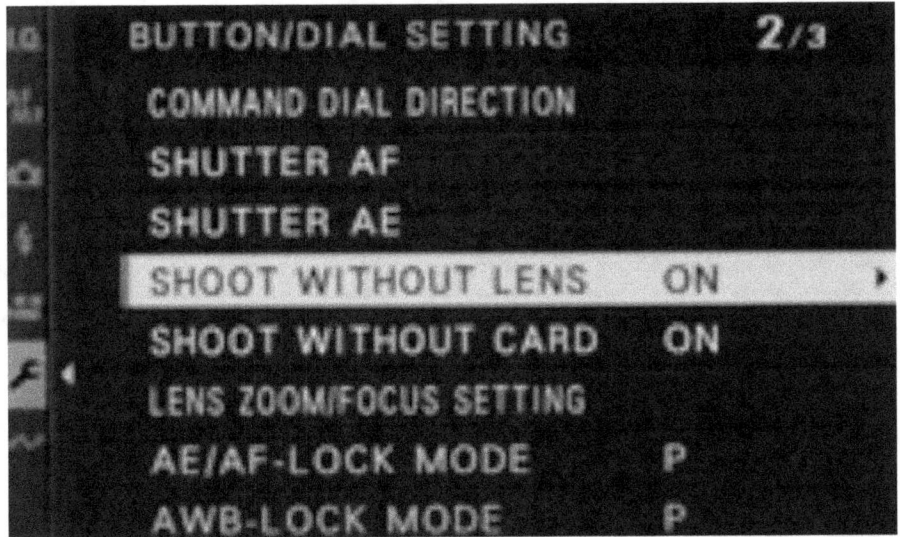

Experiment with "freelensing" or "lens whacking" by taking photos without attaching the lens directly to your camera. Hold the lens a bit away from the front of the camera to allow light to hit the sensor at various angles, creating unique light flare effects in your pictures.

Changing how you hold your camera lens can make your photos interesting. You can make certain parts of your photo clear while others are blurry. It's like using fancy lenses, but those are trickier than changing how you hold your lens. Be careful, though, because if you remove the lens, your camera can get dusty inside. If you want to take many special photos, consider getting a tilt-shift lens.

You can also turn the lens around to take super close-up shots, even if it's not a special close-up lens. The smaller the number on your lens, the closer you can get to what you're taking a picture of. But it's harder to focus if you use a wide-angle lens this way.

Exploring External Camera Features

Topside controls

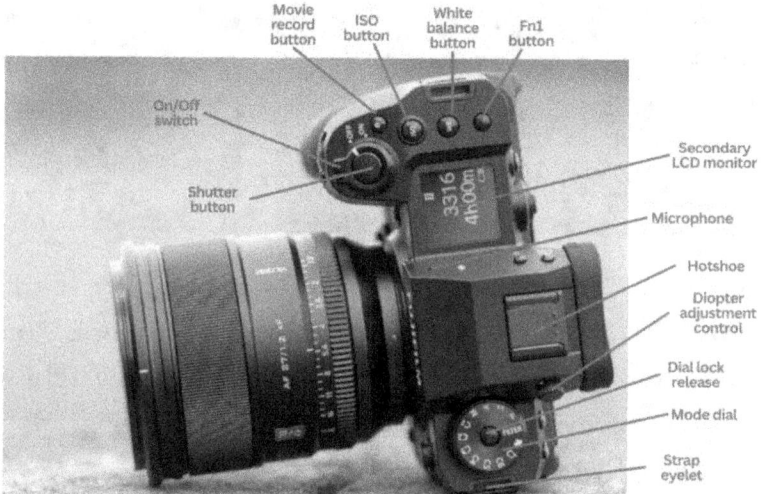

1. Mode Dial: This rotating dial lets you switch between different shooting modes, like Still Photo, Movie, Manual Exposure (M), Aperture Priority (Av), Shutter Priority (Tv), and Program Mode (P).

2. Dial Lock Release: Press this small button in the center of the Mode Dial to unlock it for rotation.

3. Shutter Button: Located in the prime position on the right side of the camera's top deck, this button captures photos when pressed halfway and takes continuous shots when held down fully.

4. Microphone: Two built-in stereo microphones flank the Mode Dial, capturing audio during movie recording.

5. Secondary LCD Monitor: This small monochrome LCD screen on the top plate displays essential shooting information like shutter speed, aperture, ISO, and battery level.

6. Power Switch: Located next to the secondary monitor, this lever turns the camera on and off.

7. Secondary Monitor Backlight Button: Press this button to illuminate the secondary LCD monitor for better visibility in low-light conditions.

8. Hotshoe: This flash shoe on the top center of the camera allows you to attach external flash units or other accessories like microphones or electronic viewfinders.

9. Video Mode Button: Dedicated for quick movie recording access, this red button on the left side of the top deck instantly starts video recording.

10. Diopter Adjustment Control: This small dial next to the viewfinder eyepiece lets you adjust the focus of the viewfinder for your eyesight.

11. Fn 1 Button: This customizable button on the left side of the top deck can be assigned various functions like white balance, focus peaking, or film simulation for quick access.

12. WB Button: Press this button on the left side of the top deck to access the white balance settings menu.

13. Image Sensor Position Mark: This small mark on the front of the camera indicates the position of the image sensor within the body, helpful for aligning certain accessories.

14. ISO Button: Located on the left side of the top deck, this button allows you to adjust the camera's ISO speed, controlling its sensitivity to light.

15. Movie Recording Button: This prominent red button on the back of the camera starts and stops movie recording.

Front features

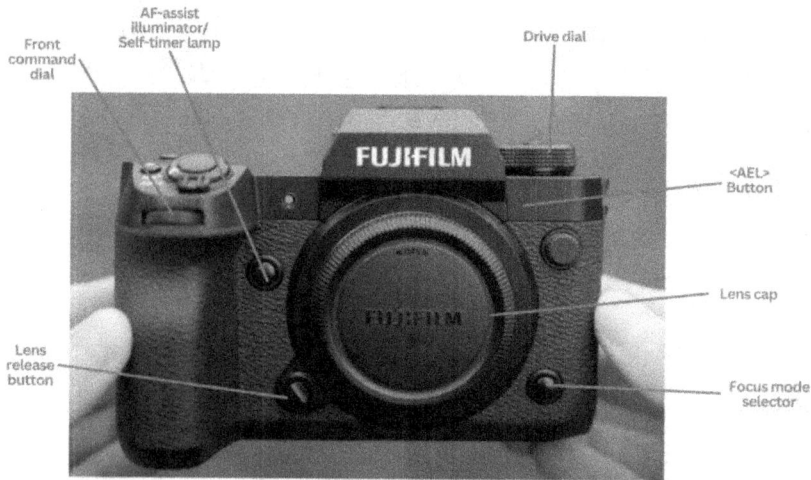

1. Front Mode Dial: This smaller dial on the front left of the lens mount lets you quickly switch between shooting modes like Single Shot, Continuous Shooting, and Self-Timer without moving your hand from the grip.

2. Fn 2 Buttons: Two customizable buttons situated near the front mode dial can be assigned various functions like focus peaking, film simulation activation, or bracketing for instant access.

3. Fn 3 Buttons: Further to the right, nestled near the lens release button, are three additional, customizable Fn 3 buttons for even more control over frequently used functions.

4. Sensor: The X-H2 boasts a powerful 40.2MP APS-C X-Trans CMOS 5 HR sensor housed behind the lens, capturing stunning detail and dynamic range in your images.

5. Sync Terminal: This port on the left side of the lens mount allows you to connect the camera to external studio flash units for precise lighting control.

6. Lens Release Button: Pressing this button disengages the lens from the camera body, enabling you to swap lenses efficiently.

7. Lens Signal Contacts: These electronic contacts transmit data between the camera and the lens, facilitating features like autofocus and aperture control.

8. Lens Fitting Mark: This red dot on the lens mount aligns with the corresponding mark on your lens for proper mounting and communication.

9. AF-Assist Illuminator / Self-Timer Light / Tally Light: This small LED assists the autofocus system in low-light conditions. It also doubles as a self-timer lamp and tally light, signaling when recording video.

10. Camera Strap Eyelet: Attach your camera strap here for secure carrying and added comfort while shooting.

11. Speaker: This built-in speaker on the right side of the lens mount lets you playback recorded audio directly from the camera.

12. Type C USB Connector: This port on the bottom serves multiple purposes: charging the battery, transferring photos and videos to your computer, and updating the camera's firmware.

13. 3.5mm Headphone Jack: Connect headphones here for real-time audio monitoring during video recording or playback.

14. 3.5mm Microphone Jack: Plug in an external microphone for high-quality audio capture to enhance your videos.

15. 2.5mm Remote Release Connector: Use a remote release cable connected here to trigger the shutter remotely, minimizing camera shake and ideal for long exposures.

16. Memory Card Slot 1 (for Type B CFexpress cards): This slot accommodates the faster Type B CFexpress cards for high-speed continuous shooting and video recording.

17. Memory Card Slot 2 (for SD memory cards): Expand your storage capacity with this SD card slot for backup or overflow photos and videos.

Back-of-the-body controls

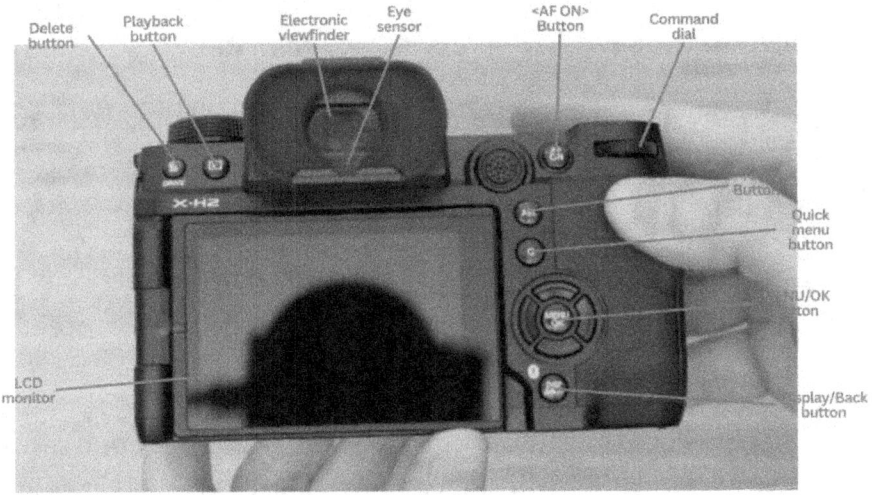

1. Drive / Delete Button: This double-duty button on the upper left corner lets you choose various shooting modes (single shot, continuous, etc.) with a short press and deletes unwanted photos or videos with a long press.

2. < ▼ > Selector Button: Use this button to navigate menus and settings downwards.

3. < ▲ > Selector Button: Navigate menus and settings upwards with this button.

4. < ► > Selector Button: Move left through menus and settings options with this button.

5. < ◄ > Selector Button: Navigate menus and settings to the right using this button.

6. Exposure Lock Button: Located near the top right corner, pressing this button locks the current exposure settings regardless of camera movement or recomposition.

7. Eye Sensor: This sensor automatically switches between the EVF and LCD monitor based on whether your eye is near the EVF, providing seamless viewing options.

8. Focus Stick: Push this joystick in eight directions to manually select your focus point within the frame for precise control.

9. Eye Cup: This soft rubber cup surrounds the EVF for a more comfortable viewing experience and blocks out extraneous light.

10. Electronic Viewfinder (EVF): This high-resolution OLED viewfinder displays your live view feed and shooting information, enabling precise framing and composition.

11. Playback Button: Located near the bottom left corner, press this button to switch to playback mode and review captured photos and videos.

12. AF-ON Button: Press this button to activate autofocus, locking focus on your subject for precise capture.

13. Quick Menu Button: Located near the bottom right corner, press this button to access frequently used settings and functions for quick adjustments without entering the full menu.

14. Indicator Lamp/Tally Light: This small light on the rear grip indicates camera status, such as whether it's recording video or connected to Wi-Fi.

15. MENU/OK Button: Press this button in the center of the four selector buttons to access the main menu or confirm selections within menus.

16. Display / Back / Bluetooth Button: Press this button to cycle through different display options on the LCD screen or return to the previous screen. Holding it down activates Bluetooth pairing.

17. Rear Command Dial: Rotate this dial to adjust settings like aperture, exposure compensation, or white balance while shooting or navigate menus for easier selection.

18. LCD Monitor / Touch Screen: This fully articulating touchscreen allows for live view monitoring, image review, and navigating menus with touch gestures for intuitive control.

19. Indicator Lamp/Tally Light (duplicate): There are actually two of these lights, one each on the rear grip and top plate, providing redundant status notifications in different viewing positions.

CHAPTER 2: FOCUSING

Focus Modes

When deciding on the focusing mode, you need to answer two questions:

1. Who will do the focusing?

Do you want the camera to focus on its own? If yes, choose either Single AF [AF-S] or Continuous AF [AF-C] mode.

Do you want to control the focus yourself? If yes, choose Manual Focus mode.

2. When will focus occur?

Should the camera focus and stay focused when you press the shutter button halfway (Single AF [AF-S])?

Or should it keep adjusting focus as long as the shutter button is pressed halfway (Continuous AF [AF-C])?

Now, let's look at the three focus modes to choose from: [AF-S], [AF-C], and [MF].

To set the Focus mode, follow these steps:

1. Go to the <MENU>, then choose [AF/MF], and finally, select [FOCUS MODE] for still images.

2. Similarly, navigate to <MENU>, [AF/MF], and [FOCUS MODE] for movie recording.

3. Choose one of the following options:

- **[MF] MANUAL FOCUS:** Adjust the focus manually using the lens focus ring.

- **[AF-C] CONTINUOUS AF:** Continuous focus adjustment while holding the shutter button halfway.

- **[AF-S] SINGLE AF:** Set and lock focus when pressing the shutter button halfway.

Single Auto Focus

Single AF, or AF-S, is for still subjects like landscapes or posed portraits. With [AF-S], the camera focuses when you press the shutter button halfway and stays fixed while you keep it pressed halfway.

Continuous Auto Focus

Continuous AF, or AF-C, helps you capture things always on the go, like cars or sports. When you hold the shutter button halfway, the camera keeps adjusting the focus to follow the moving subject and guesses where it will be when you take the photo.

Imagine taking a photo of someone walking towards you. If you use AF-S, the camera focuses when you press halfway, but if the person gets closer, they might become blurry. With AF-C, the camera keeps adjusting focus as the person moves, making them more likely to stay focused.

Manual Focus

Finally, there's manual focus. You have to set the focus yourself because the camera won't do it for you. It is useful for videos or when the autofocus isn't getting the right focus on what you want. Just turn the focus ring on the lens to do manual focus.

Auto Focus Mode

If you picked [AF-S] or [AF-C] for the Focus Mode, you should choose where the camera focuses. If it's focusing on the wrong thing, adjust the autofocus area. The camera uses focus points to find contrasting areas and focus on them.

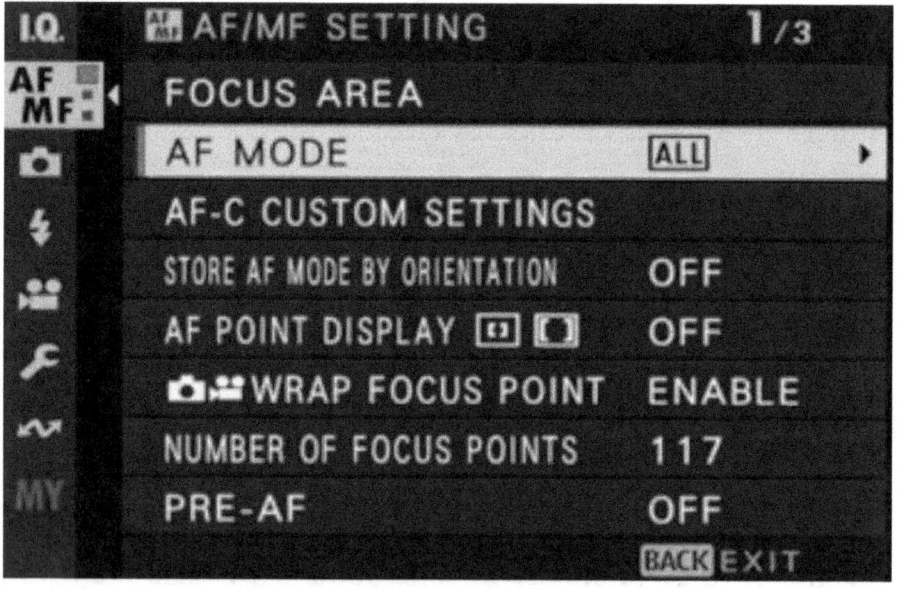

Now, let's explore the autofocus options.

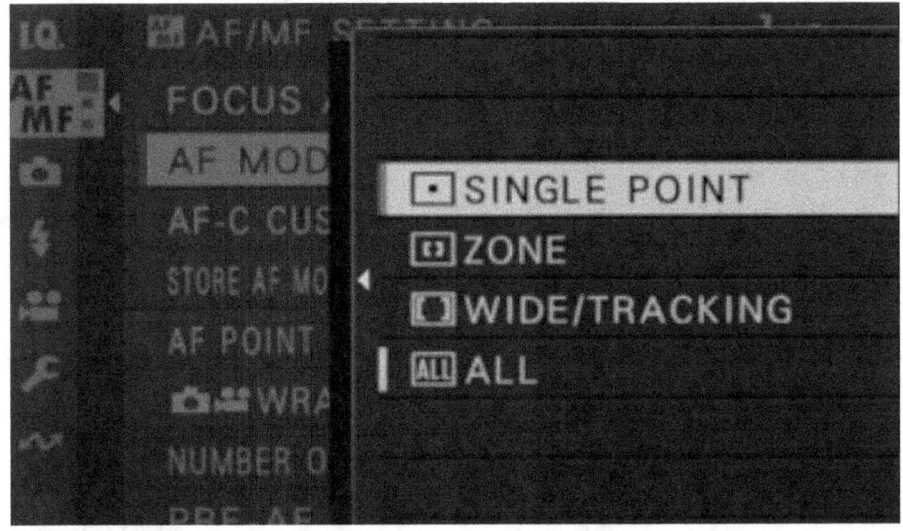

Single Point

Choose where you want the camera to focus by moving a point on the screen. Adjust the focus point by tilting the stick and changing its size by rotating the dial. Using Continuous AF mode, the camera will track the subject at the chosen focus point, ideal for moving subjects.

Zone

The camera divides the picture into sections to help focus on things. Each section can have many focus points, and you can adjust them using the focus stick. Change the section size by turning the dial. When in [AF-C] Continuous AF mode, the camera follows and focuses on the subject in that section, which is great for moving subjects with a predictable path.

Wide/Tracking

The camera focuses on things with strong contrasts in the whole picture. It uses all the focus points to find the sharp areas, and you'll see green frames showing where it's focusing. If you set it to [AF-C] Continuous AF, the camera will follow a moving subject in the frame.

All

If you choose "All," you can use the back dial to cycle through focus modes: Single Point, Zone, and Wide/Tracking.

Selecting an Auto Focus Mode

Choose the focus mode by navigating the menu: [AF/MF] and then select [AF MODE].

Focus Area

After choosing the autofocus mode, you can decide where the camera should focus by selecting specific points. To help you visualize this, turn on the focus point display, which shows a grid of small squares representing the focus points.

I.Q.	AF/MF SETTING	1/3

FOCUS AREA

AF MODE	ALL
AF-C CUSTOM SETTINGS	
STORE AF MODE BY ORIENTATION	OFF
AF POINT DISPLAY	OFF
WRAP FOCUS POINT	ENABLE
NUMBER OF FOCUS POINTS	117
PRE-AF	OFF

A green frame may appear, indicating where the camera will search for subjects based on contrast. Adjust the focus frame's position and size using the focus stick and rear command dial. It determines where the camera focuses on objects.

AF Point Display

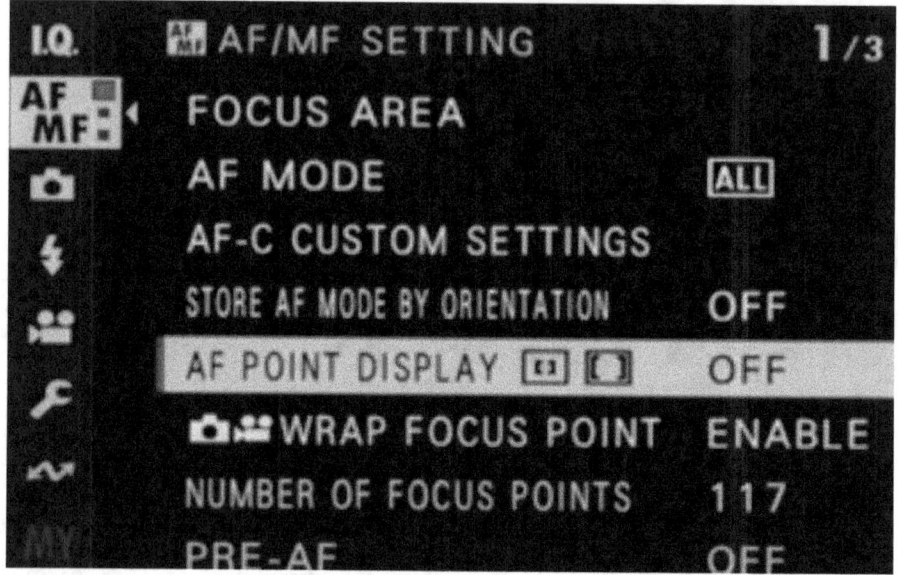

To show or hide the focus points on your camera, go to <MENU> → [AF/MF] → [AF MODE] and choose [Wide]/[Tracking] or [Zone]. Then, to turn focus point display on or off, navigate to <MENU> → [AF/MF] → [AF POINT DISPLAY] and select [ON] to display focus points or [OFF] to hide them.

Number of Focus Points

When manually focusing or using the [SINGLE POINT] autofocus mode, you can choose how many focus points are available.

To set the number of focus points:

1. Go to <MENU> → [AF/MF] → [NUMBER OF FOCUS POINTS]

2. Choose:

   - **[117 POINTS (9X13)]:** Pick from 117 focus points in a 9 x 13 grid

   - **[425 POINTS (17 x 25)]:** Choose from 425 focus points in a 17 x 25 grid

Pre-AF

Set the camera to focus ahead of time for quicker operation. When the camera is steady, it can focus while you wait to capture the perfect shot. Pressing the shutter button after focusing in advance makes the focus adjustment faster. Keep in mind that focusing ahead of time uses more battery. With [PRE-AF] set to [ON], the focus keeps adjusting in [AF-S] and [AF-C] even without pressing the shutter button.

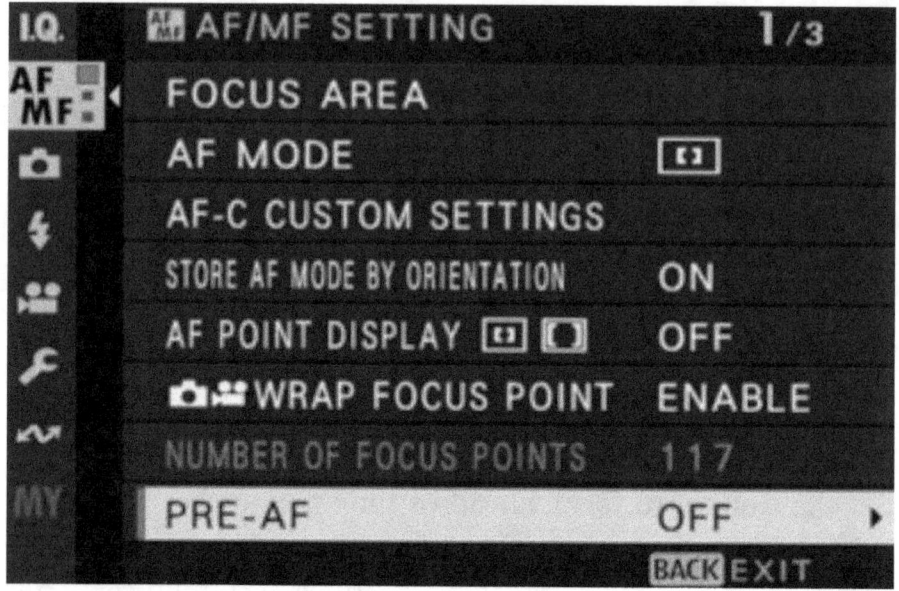

Enabling/Disabling Pre-AF

Choose "MENU," then go to "AF/MF," followed by "PRE-AF," and decide between turning it "ON" or "OFF."

Store AF Mode By Orientation

If you often switch between holding your camera upright and sideways, use the [STORE AF MODE BY ORIENTATION] Setting. This feature remembers the focus settings you used for portrait (upright) and landscape (sideways) shots. For example, if you set [STORE AF MODE BY ORIENTATION] to [ON], when you shoot sideways (landscape), you might use Single Point AF Mode with the focus point in the upper right. Then, when you turn the camera upright (portrait), it remembers to switch to Zone AF Mode with the focus point in the upper right.

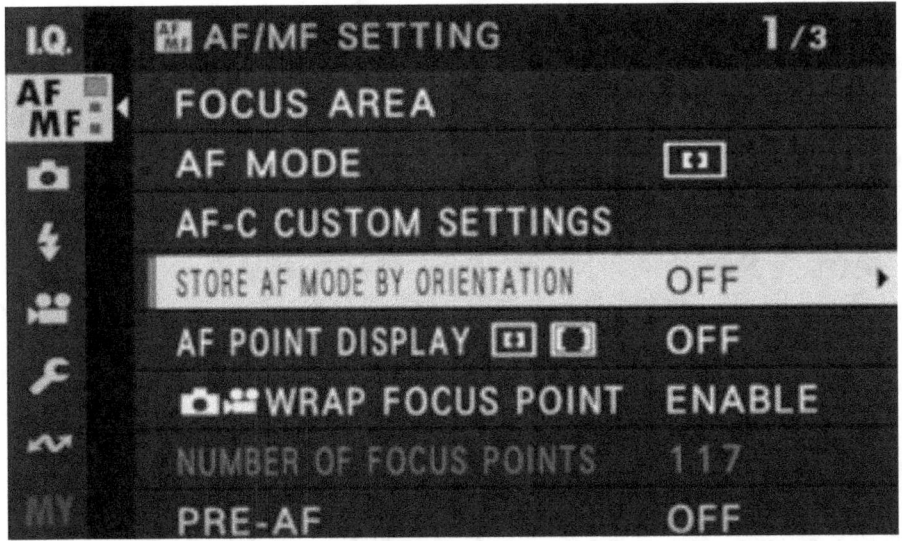

When you turn the camera, it remembers where you focused and how in each direction. If you turn it horizontally (landscape), the focus point goes to the upper right; if vertically (portrait), it goes to the lower right and changes focus type.

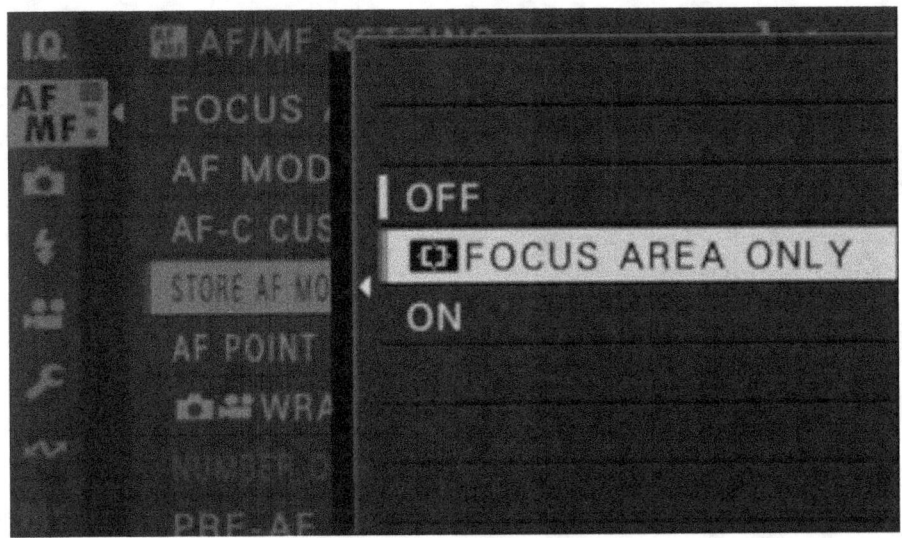

But, if you choose only to save the focus area preference in the landscape, it stays in the upper right. When you turn it to portrait, the focus point moves to the lower right, but the focus type doesn't change.

Setting Store AF Mode by Orientation

1. Go to the menu, choose between auto-focus (AF) and manual focus (MF), then select an option to save focus settings based on the camera orientation.

2. Choose:

   - **[OFF]:** Keep the focus settings constant regardless of the camera orientation.

   - **[FOCUS AREA ONLY]:** Let the focus area move with the camera orientation, but keep the focus mode the same.

   - **[ON]:** Allow focus mode and focus frame position to adjust based on the camera's orientation.

Back Button Focus

If you choose an autofocus, you might wonder how you want the camera to focus automatically. Usually, when you press the shutter button halfway, the camera meters and focuses, and when fully pressed, it takes a picture. So, the default autofocus method is to use the shutter button.

But wait, there's another way! Some photographers like to split the focus from the button that takes the picture. Instead of the shutter button, they use the <AF ON> button to focus. It's called back button focus, which means you focus by pressing <AF ON> instead of the shutter button.

With back button focus, you can quickly switch between autofocus and manual focus. Press the <AF ON> button to autofocus, and don't press it to keep your focus without the camera autofocus.

Back button focus makes taking pictures faster by separating the focusing step from pressing the shutter button. Instead of relying on autofocus when you press the shutter button, you preset the focus by pressing the <AF ON> button. It ensures a quicker shot without the risk of autofocus issues, and to set it up, turn off [SHUTTER AF] for both [AF-S] and [AF-C].

Setting Shutter AF

- Go to the menu, navigate the AF/MF settings, then select Button/Dial Setting and Shutter AF.

- Choose the focus mode:

- o For AF-S mode:

  - ■ **ON:** Press halfway to lock focus.

  - ■ **OFF:** No autofocus when pressing halfway.

- o For AF-C mode:

  - ■ **ON:** The camera keeps focusing while the button is halfway pressed.

  - ■ **OFF:** No autofocus when pressing halfway.

How to Take a Picture with Back Button Focus

1. Use the <AF-ON> button to ensure your camera focuses on the subject automatically.

2. Press the shutter button to capture the photo.

Subject Detection

1. The X-H2 can identify people, animals, and vehicles. You can turn on/off subject detection for photos by going to <MENU> → [AF/MF] → [SUBJECT DETECTION SETTING]. For videos, follow the same steps.

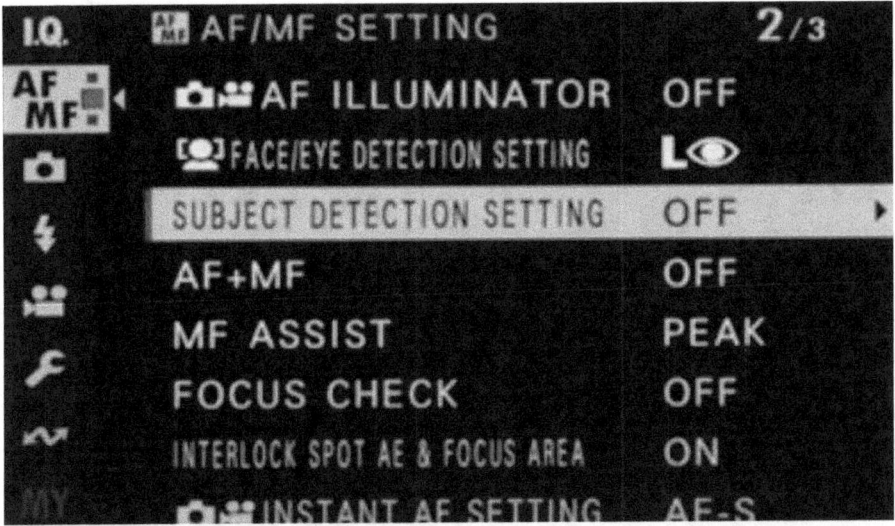

2. Choose what the camera focuses on:

- ANIMAL: The camera focuses on and tracks dogs and cats.

- BIRD: The camera focuses on and tracks birds.

- AUTOMOBILE: The camera focuses on and tracks the bodies and front ends of cars, especially racing cars.

- MOTORCYCLE & BIKE: The camera focuses on and tracks riders of motorcycles and bicycles.

39

- AIRPLANE: The camera focuses on and tracks cockpits, noses, or bodies of airplanes.

- TRAIN: The camera focuses on and tracks driver compartments or front ends of trains.

- [OFF]: The camera doesn't prioritize animals or vehicles for focus.

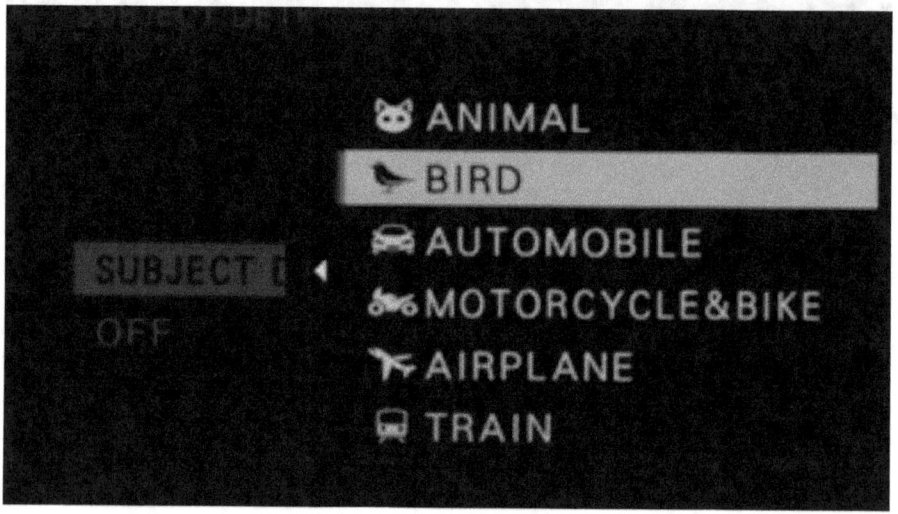

Manual Focus

When you use manual focusing, you, the person operating the camera, are the one in charge of adjusting the focus. This is different from letting the camera automatically do it for you. This manual control comes in handy, especially when you're shooting videos.

When the camera relies on automatic focus, it might cause the image to shake as it tries to refocus. But with manual focus, you have more control, which can result in smoother and more visually pleasing videos. You get to decide when and how the focus changes, making your footage look better overall.

Using Manual Focus

1. For photos, go to the menu, select AF/MF, then FOCUS MODE, and finally MF. For videos, follow the same steps.

2. Turn the focus ring on the lens to adjust the focus.

Turn the focus ring on the lens to focus manually. Twist it left to make things closer; twist it right to make them farther away. You can switch this if you want.

Setting the Focus Ring Direction

To adjust the focus on your X-H2 camera:

1. Go to the menu and navigate to AF/MF > Button/Dial Setting> Lens Zoom/Focus Setting > Focus Ring Rotate.

2. Choose:

   - CW: Turn the focus ring clockwise to increase the focus distance.

   - CCW: Turn the focus ring counterclockwise to increase the focus distance.

The X-H2 also lets you pick how focus changes when you rotate the focus ring.

Setting the Focus Ring Operation

1. Go to the camera menu, choose AF/MF, then navigate to Button/Dial Setting, Lens Zoom/Focus Setting, and Focus Ring Operation.

2. Choose between two options:

   - **Nonlinear:** Focus changes in sync with how much you turn the focus ring.

   - **Linear:** Focus adjusts based on ring rotation, but the speed isn't tied to how fast you turn the ring.

If you want a manual focus indicator on the screen, ensure the Manual Focus Distance Indicator is enabled in Menu > Setting icon > Screen Set-up > Disp. Custom Setting.

The manual focus indicator tells you how well your camera is focused on the subject. The white line shows how far your subject is (meters or feet). The blue bar indicates the range in front and behind the subject that will be in focus. If you're using autofocus, a similar indicator called AF DISTANCE INDICATOR can be turned on in the settings.

Setting the Depth-of-Field Scale

- Go to the menu, choose AD/MF, and then find the Depth-of-Field Scale option.

- Choose either a Pixel Basis to adjust the depth of field for high-resolution electronic displays or a Film Format Basis for prints.

Manual Focus Assist

The X-H2 has tools to help you focus precisely when manually adjusting the focus. You can find these tools in the [MF Assist] menu, and the selected tool determines how the screen looks in manual focus mode.

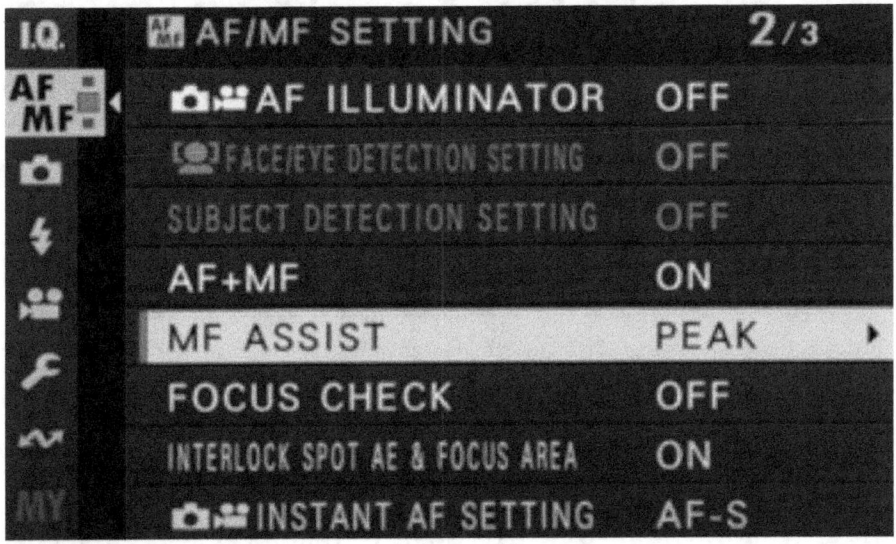

Digital Split Image

Digital Split Image is a feature that makes focusing easier. Imagine your camera screen having a split image in the middle, either in black and white or color. If it's black and white, it's simpler and helps you focus better by reducing distractions.

When your picture is not focused, the lines in the split image break apart. But when it's in focus, the lines align, creating a pattern like a checkerboard. This feature is especially useful when you're taking pictures with lots of lines, making sure everything looks sharp and clear.

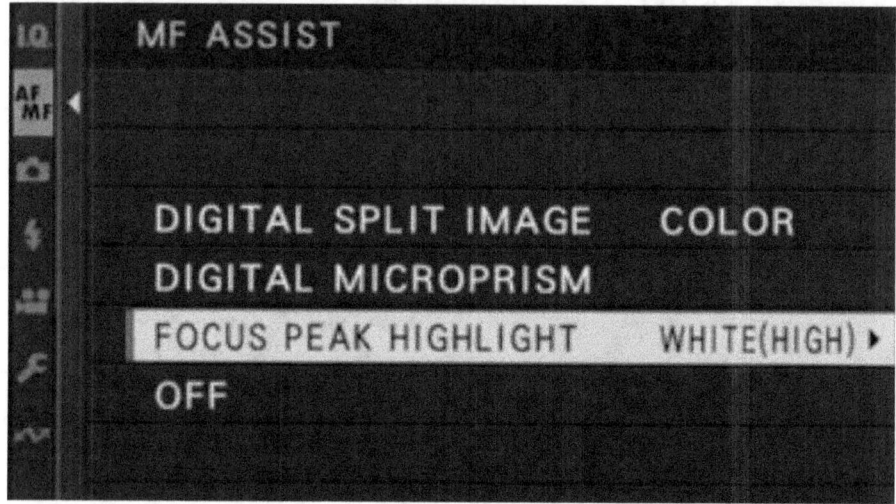

Digital Microprism

Digital Microprism is another helpful tool for focusing. It places a grid in the middle of your picture. When something is blurry, the grid shows it more clearly. So, if your subject is not in focus, the grid will look fuzzy.

But when your subject is clear and in focus, the blurry grid transforms into a sharp and clear picture. This feature is great for making sure your subjects are crisp and well-defined in your photos.

Focus PeakHighlight

When you turn on the focus peak highlight on your camera, something cool happens! The camera kind of draws lines around the things it believes are in focus. These lines are bold and easy to see because they have high contrast. It's like the camera is saying, "Hey, look, I think these things are sharp and clear!"

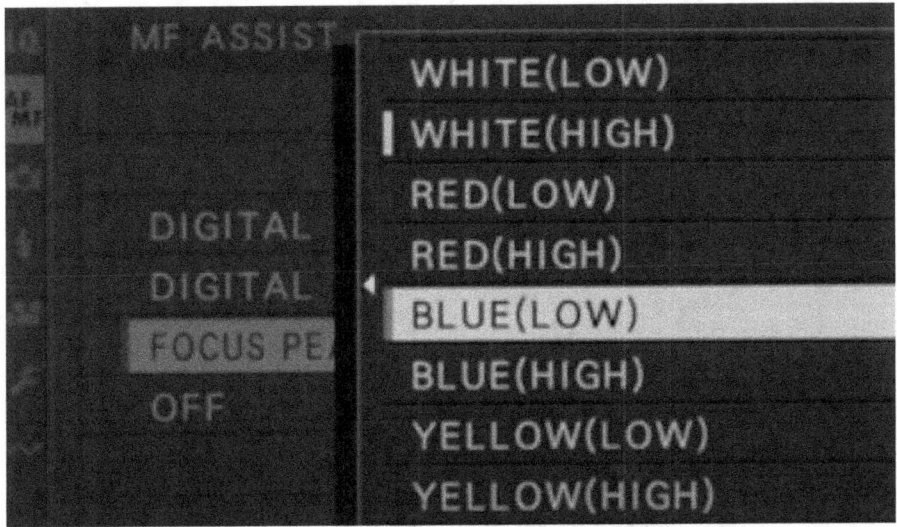

But here's the really neat part: these lines don't actually show up in the pictures or videos you take. They're just there to help you while you're setting up your shot. So, you get this handy guide to know what your camera thinks is in focus, without it affecting your final photo or video. It's like having a helpful friend who points out the important stuff without leaving any marks behind!

You can pick the color and how sensitive this highlighting is. Low sensitivity means only clear focus gets highlighted, while high sensitivity means more things get outlined because it needs less contrast.

Selecting How Focus is Displayed in Manual Focus Mode for Still Images

1. Choose <MENU>, then go to [AF/MF], followed by [MF ASSIST]. From the options below, pick one :

    - **[DIGITAL SPLIT IMAGE]:** Shows a split image in the middle of the frame.

    - **[MONOCHROME]:** The split image is in black and white.

    - **[COLOR]:** The split image is in color.

    - **[DIGITAL MICROPRISM]:** Displays a grid pattern that highlights blur when the subject is out of focus.

    - **[FOCUS PEAK HIGHLIGHT]:** Emphasizes high contrast outlines. Choose a peaking color and sensitivity.

    - **[OFF]:** Focus is usually displayed without digital split image, microprism, or peaking.

The X-H2 has helpful features for recording videos with manual focus. It has focus peaking, which works like it does for photos. A focus meter also looks like a speedometer below the focus point. If the needle points left, the focus is in front of the subject; if it points right, the focus is behind. When the needle points straight up, and the meter turns green, the camera is focused on the subject within the focus point.

Configuring Manual Focus Assist for Movie Recording

1. Go to the menu, choose [AF/MF], then select [MF ASSIST].

2. Choose from these focus options:

   - **[FOCUS PEAK HIGHLIGHT]:** Highlights high-contrast outlines with a chosen color and level.

   - **[FOCUS METER]:** A needle display indicates whether the focus is in front or behind the subject.

   - **[FOCUS METER + PEAK HIGHLIGHT]:** Displays focus peaking and focus meter assist tools.

   - **[OFF]:** Disables focus peaking, and the camera usually displays.

Image Stabilization

Image stabilization, as exemplified by the advanced technology integrated into the X-H2 camera, serves as a crucial feature that significantly enhances the quality of your photos and videos. When capturing still images, this technology plays a key role in reducing the impact of shaky hands or subtle movements, resulting in clearer and sharper photographs. In simpler terms, it helps eliminate the blurriness that can occur due to the inherent instability of human hand movements during photography.

Furthermore, image stabilization extends its benefits to video recording by ensuring a smooth and steady footage. This is particularly valuable in preventing the onset of motion sickness for viewers, as the stabilized visuals eliminate the jarring effects caused by abrupt camera movements. In essence, whether you are capturing a scenic landscape or recording dynamic moments, the image stabilization feature contributes to an overall more enjoyable and professional-looking viewing experience.

Configuring Image Stabilization for Still Photography

1. Go to the menu and choose either Auto Focus (AF) or Manual Focus (MF), then select the Image Stabilization (IS) mode.

2. Choose one of the following options:

   - **Continuous:** Keeps image stabilization always on.

   - **Shooting Only:** Activates image stabilization when you press the shutter button halfway or release it in focus mode (AF-C).

- **Off:** Turns off image stabilization, which is useful when using a tripod or stable surface.

Configuring Image Stabilization for Movie Recording

1. Choose [AF/MF] and then [IS MODE] from the menu.

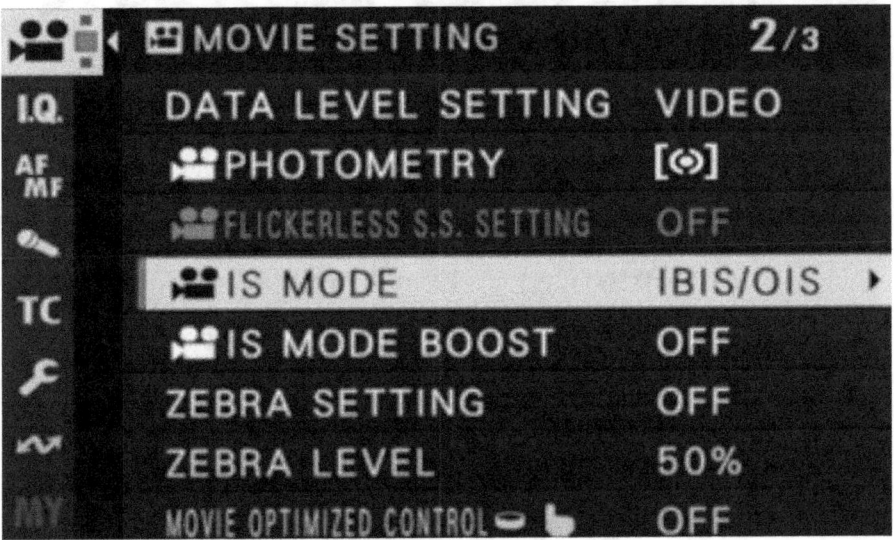

2. Select one of the following:

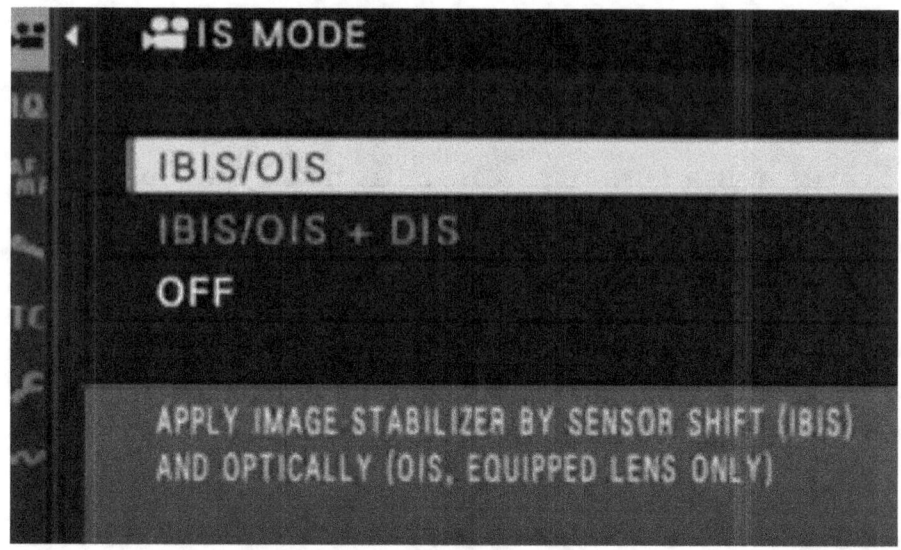

- **[IBIS/OIS]**: Use both in-body image stabilization (IBIS) and optical image stabilization (OIS). IBIS is for lenses without OIS.

- **[IBIS/OIS + DIS]:** Enable IBIS, OIS, and digital image stabilization (DIS). The crop adjusts based on settings in <MENU> → [Camera icon] → [MOVIE MODE].

- **[OFF]:** Turn off image stabilization with a tripod or stable surface.

If your lens has a stabilizer switch, the Setting on the lens will take priority over the menu setting. There's also an option called "IS MODE BOOST" that enhances image stabilization, which is handy when shooting without a tripod to reduce camera shake and create a steadier shot.

Chapter 3: Choosing Basic Picture Settings

Drive Settings

The drive mode is like giving orders to the camera when you press the button to take a picture. Press the <DRIVE>/<Delete> button to choose how you want it to behave.

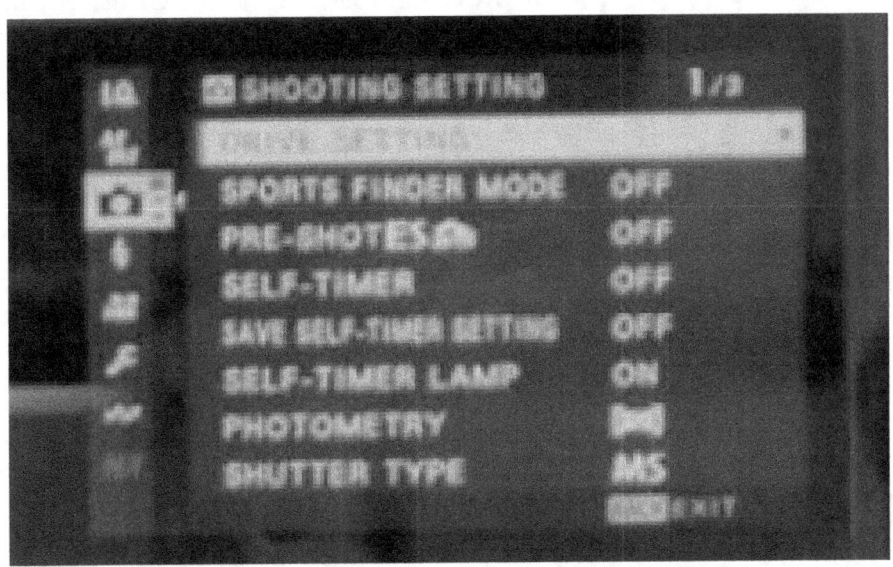

Selecting a Drive Mode

1. Click the <DRIVE> button for different photo modes:

   - **Single frame:** Takes one picture when you press the button.

   - **High-speed burst:** Takes many pictures quickly while holding the button.

- **Low-speed burst:** Takes consecutive pictures at a slower rate than high-speed burst.

- **[ISO] ISO BKT:** Captures images with different ISO settings.

- **[WB] WHITE BALANCE BKT:** Captures images with different white balance settings.

- **[BKT] Bracket:** Choose AE, Film Simulation, Dynamic Range, or Focus Bracketing.

- **[HDR]:** Captures a high dynamic range image.

- **Panorama:** Captures a wide-angle image.

- **Multiple Exposure:** Combines multiple shots.

- **PIXEL SHIFT MULTI SHOT:** Takes shots for a high-resolution RAW image.

Continuous Shooting Drive Modes

Continuous shooting on your camera is like taking lots of pictures one after another when you press and hold the button that makes the camera take a photo. It stops taking pictures when you let go of the button. This is really useful when things are happening fast, like a race or a dancing party, and you're not sure exactly when the best moment will happen. It's also good for making a set of pictures that show something moving.

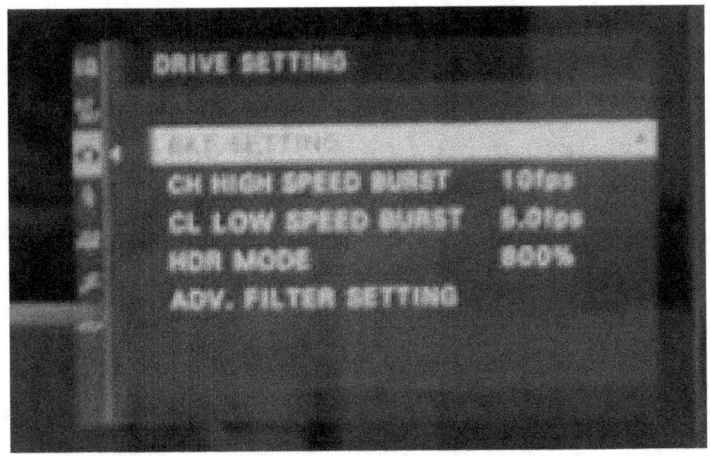

The X-H2 camera lets you choose how fast you want it to take these pictures. There are two options: fast (CH HIGH-SPEED BURST) and slower (CL LOW-SPEED BURST). "Fast" means the camera takes pictures quickly one after another, while "slower" means it takes them a bit more slowly. The speed is like how fast the pictures happen, and it's called the frame rate. If you choose CH HIGH-SPEED BURST, the camera takes pictures faster than CL LOW-SPEED BURST. But, you should know that with the fast way, you might not see what's happening right away on the screen as you take pictures. If you want to see things better while taking pictures, you can pick one of the slower options, like CL LOW SPEED BURST.

Sometimes, if you take a lot of pictures in a row, the camera might slow down a bit. Also, by default, all the pictures in the quick series will look the same, with the same brightness. But, if you want each picture to be a bit different, you can go to the camera's menu, pick settings, then button or dial settings, and turn off something called shutter AE. This way, each picture can have its own special brightness.

Configuring Continuous Shooting

1. Push the <DRIVE> button.

2. Select:

    *   Choose a speed for taking pictures:

        *   **[20fps (1.29X CROP)]:** Takes 20 pictures per second with a 1.29x crop and only works with the electronic shutter.

        *   **[13fps (1.29X CROP)]:** Takes 13 pictures per second with a 1.29x crop, only works with electronic shutter.

        *   **[10 fps(1.29X CROP)]:** Takes 10 pictures per second with a 1.29x crop, only works with electronic shutter.

        *   **[15fps]:** Takes 15 pictures per second with a mechanical shutter or 13 pictures per second with an electronic shutter.

        *   **[10fps]:** Takes 10 pictures per second with a mechanical shutter or 8.9 pictures per second with an electronic shutter.

    *   Choose one of the following:

- **[7.0fps]:** Takes 7 pictures per second with a mechanical shutter or 6.7 pictures per second with an electronic shutter.

- **[5.0fps]:** Takes 5 pictures per second.

- **[3.0fps]:** Takes 3 pictures per second.

Shutter Type

The Fuji X-H2 lets you choose how it takes pictures. You can pick the regular way with a mechanical shutter, just like in those big DSLR cameras. This shutter has curtains that open and close to catch the light for the picture. Or, you can use an electronic shutter or let the camera decide what's best for the situation.

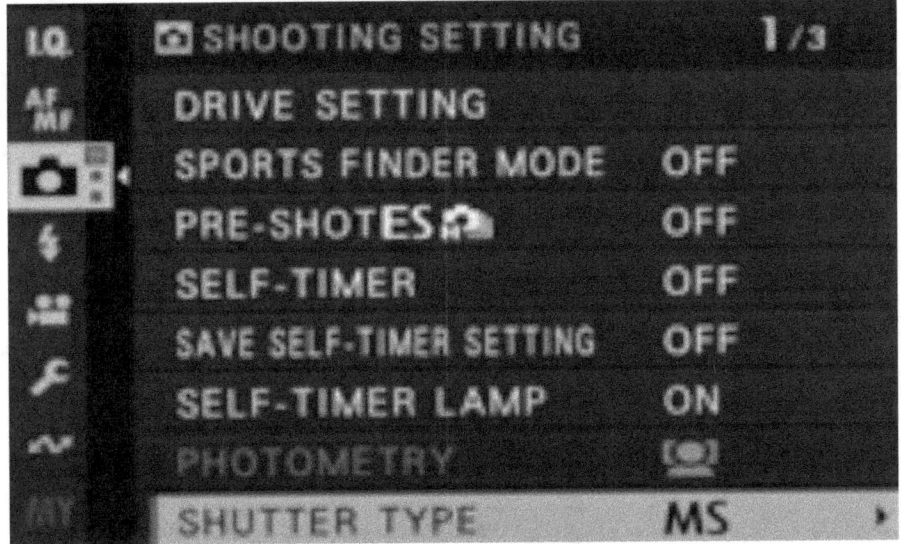

Now, the electronic shutter is like a magic switch for the camera sensor. It turns on and off to take pictures without any moving parts, which means it's super quiet, stops the camera from shaking, and takes pictures faster than the regular shutter.

But here's the thing: using the electronic shutter might make pictures look a bit strange, especially when things are moving fast or the light is changing, like when you use a flash. It's like the camera takes different parts of the picture at different times. Imagine a garage door going up and down – the camera starts at the top, gets sensitive to light, reads one line at a time, and moves down until the whole picture is taken.

Usually, this happens really fast, and we don't even notice. But when you move the camera quickly or capture super-fast things, like an airplane propeller, the picture might wobble, like jello (that's why it's called the jello effect), and straight lines can look a little bent and twisted.

Using an electronic shutter in artificial light can cause another problem. The lights flicker very quickly, too fast for us to see. When a camera with an electronic shutter captures this, it might make parts of the photo too bright or dark, creating a striped pattern. That's also why you can't use a flash with an electronic shutter. The flash is so quick that it might only light up certain parts of the photo, depending on when the camera reads the sensor.

To capture fast-moving things, pan, or shoot in artificial light with a flash, use the mechanical shutter on the Fuji X-H2. There's also a mode called E-Front Curtain Shutter (EF) that mixes electronic and mechanical shutters. EF helps stop the camera from shaking and distortion by starting with an electronic shutter and finishing with a mechanical one. Remember, EF isn't completely silent and has some limits on high shutter speeds and flash photography.

Selecting a Shutter Type

1. Choose the camera icon on the menu, then pick the shutter type.

2. Options:

   - **Mechanical Shutter:** Only uses the mechanical shutter.

   - **Electronic Shutter:** Only uses the electronic shutter.

   - **E-Front Curtain Shutter:** Starts exposure with electronic shutter and ends with mechanical shutter.

   - **Mechanical + Electronic:** Automatically switches between mechanical and electronic shutter based on speed and conditions.

   - **E-Front + Mechanical:** Automatically switches between E-Front curtain and mechanical shutter based on speed and conditions.

   - **E-Front + Mechanical + Electronic:** Automatically selects mechanical, electronic, or

E-Front curtain shutter based on speed and conditions.

ISO BKT

When you take a picture with your camera, there's a cool thing called ISO bracketing. It's like magic for your photos! So, when you press the button to take a photo, the camera actually takes three pictures at the same time. Imagine it like making two extra copies of your drawing. Now, let's talk about ISO. ISO is like how bright or dark your photo is.

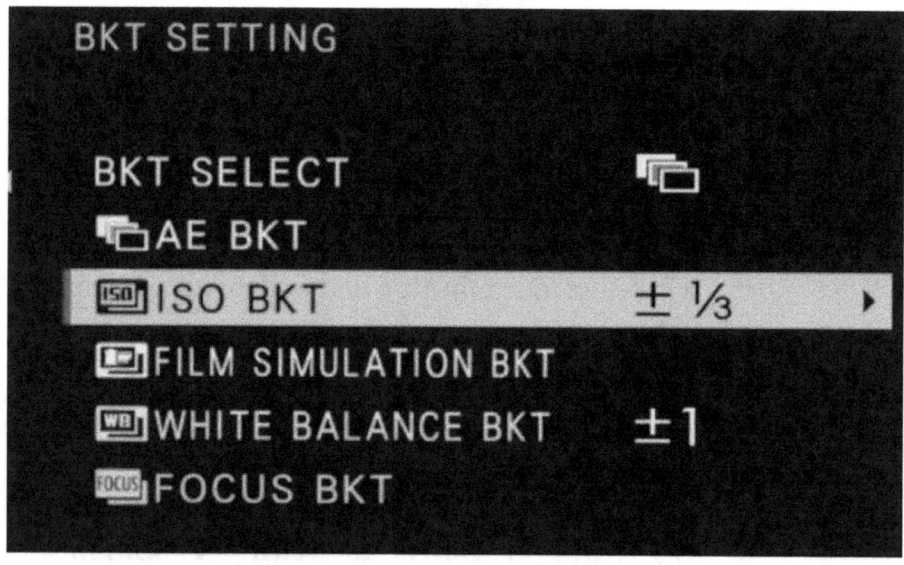

With ISO bracketing, the camera makes one photo at the brightness you picked (let's say 400), one a bit darker (200), and one a bit brighter (800). It's like having three different flavors of ice cream – one normal, one a little less sweet, and one a little extra sweet. So, when you look at your pictures later, you can pick the one that looks just right, like choosing your favorite ice cream! And that's how ISO bracketing makes your photos extra special!

Using ISO Bracketing

1. Push the <DRIVE> button and pick [ISO BKT].

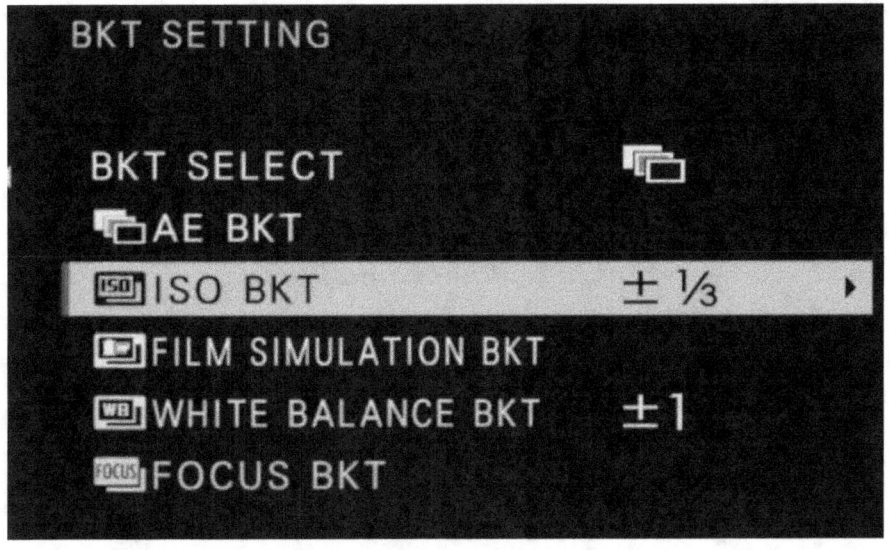

2. Choose how much difference you want: a little [+-1/3], a bit more [+-2/3], or a lot [+-1].

3. Take a picture, and you'll get three images with different ISO settings.

Paranorma

When you take pictures with your camera, the lens is like the eye of the camera, and sometimes it can't see everything in one go. Imagine you want to capture a really wide scene, like a beautiful landscape or a big group of friends. But, oh no! The lens is not wide enough to fit it all in one picture. That's when something called "panorama" comes to the rescue!

Panorama is like putting puzzle pieces together to make a big picture. With the X-H2 camera, there's a special mode just for panoramas. It's like having a helper who automatically takes different pictures from different angles and stitches them together to make a super cool, extra-wide photo. So, even if your lens can't capture everything in one shot, the panorama mode helps you create a picture that shows the whole amazing scene!

Taking a Panorama Photo

1. Tap the <DRIVE> button and pick [] PANORAMA.

2. Use the <◄> button to set your photo's width, then press <MENU/OK>.

3. Use the <►> button to pick which way your photo will pan, then press <MENU/OK>.

4. Stand with your feet pointing to the middle of your photo.

Turn your upper body as far as possible, or use a tripod. Press and hold the shutter button while turning toward the arrow on the screen to start the panorama. Let go of the button, and the camera will stop automatically when it reaches the end of the on-screen guide.

Try this fun idea for panoramic photos: Have a friend take a wide photo from left to right. Stand still in one place, and as the camera pans, quickly move behind your friend and pose again. You'll end up with a cool panorama showing you in different positions.

HDR

Cameras are really smart, but sometimes they get a bit confused when there's too much brightness in a photo. Imagine taking a picture with a big, bright window behind someone. Uh-oh! The person might look too dark, or the window is too, too bright. It's like the camera is trying to do two things at once and finding it a bit tricky.

Now, here's the cool part. If some parts of the picture are super bright, and others are really dark, the camera can ask for help. It uses something called HDR, which stands for High Dynamic Range. HDR is like a superhero move for the camera!

What happens is, the camera takes not just one picture, but three! One picture is for what the camera thinks is just right, another for the super dark spots to see all the details there, and a third for the super bright spots. Then, like magic, these pictures come together to make one awesome photo that shows all the cool details in both the bright and dark places.

When the camera is taking these special pictures, it's important to keep it very still. Imagine it's doing a little dance, but the dance has to be super still, so the pictures fit together perfectly. Just remember, the final picture might be a bit smaller, like a mini version, because it's working hard to keep all the details and make a fantastic photo!

Shooting HDR

1. Push the <DRIVE> button, choose [BKT], then pick [HDR].

2. Choose one of these options:

   - **[HDR AUTO]:** The camera automatically picks HDR from 200% to 800%.

   - **[HDR200]:** Set dynamic range to 200%.

   - **[HDR400]:** Set dynamic range to 400%.

   - **[HDR800]:** Set dynamic range to 800%.

   - **[HDR800+]:** Maximum dynamic range variation.

3. Press the shutter button to take a series of pictures that will be merged into a single final image.

Setting Resolution and File Type (The Image Quality Setting)

Image Quality

You can choose how much to shrink images, focusing on either keeping them looking good or making the file smaller.

I.Q.	IO IMAGE QUALITY SETTING	1/4
AF MF	IMAGE SIZE	L 3:2
📷	IMAGE QUALITY	F+RAW
🔦	RAW RECORDING	LOSSLESS
📹	SELECT JPEG/HEIF	HEIF
🔧	FILM SIMULATION	
〰	MONOCHROMATIC COLOR	WC 0 MG 0
	GRAIN EFFECT	OFF
MY	COLOR CHROME EFFECT	OFF

RAW vs. JPEG vs HEIF

When you take pictures, there are three special ways to save them: RAW, JPEG, and HEIF. Let's talk about each one!

First, there's RAW. It's like having super-detailed pictures, but they take up more space on your camera or computer. If you want to edit your photos later and make them look even more amazing, RAW is the way to go. Fujifilm uses ".RAF" for their RAW files, but not all computer programs can understand them. If you have a Fujifilm camera, you can use special software called Image Data Converter to edit your RAW pictures. But be careful, some camera tricks, like [Auto HDR], don't work when you use RAW.

Then there's JPEG. It's like the friendly helper that works with almost every device. JPEG pictures are a bit smaller, so they're easy to share and show on your phone, computer, or even your TV.

Lastly, there's HEIF. It makes tiny files that look really, really good! The X-H2 camera saves HEIF pictures as ".HIF," but to see them on a computer, you have to change the ending to ".HEIC." Don't worry; when you connect your camera to the computer with a special cord called USB, it does this changing all by itself.

Adjusting Image Quality:

1. Go to <MENU>, then select [I.Q] and [IMAGE QUALITY].

2. Choose:

   - **[FINE]:** Records high-quality images with low compression.

   - **[NORMAL]:** Records images with higher compression, allowing more storage.

   - **[FINE + RAW]:** Records both RAW and fine-quality JPEG or HEIF images.

   - **[NORMAL + RAW]:** Records both RAW and normal-quality JPEG or HEIF images.

   - **[RAW]:** Records only a RAW file.

3. To decide between JPEG and HEIF format, follow the given instructions.

RAW Image

To seamlessly toggle between capturing images in RAW format or an alternative format, you can utilize a designated function button on your camera. By assigning the [RAW] item to this specific button, you gain the flexibility to dynamically adjust your camera settings with a single press.

Upon pressing the assigned function button for the first time, the camera intelligently transitions into RAW image capture mode, optimizing settings to capture images in their highest quality and retaining maximum detail. Subsequently, pressing the button again triggers an automatic reversion to the original settings, providing a swift and convenient means to switch between RAW and alternate image formats effortlessly.

This innovative feature not only empowers photographers with granular control over their output but also streamlines the process, allowing them to focus on their creative vision without the need for extensive menu navigation or setting adjustments. The tactile and responsive nature of the function button enhances the overall user experience, making it a valuable tool for photographers who prioritize both efficiency and image quality in their work.

Currently selected option for [IMAGE QUALITY]	Behavior when [RAW] function button is pressed
FINE	FINE + RAW
NORMAL	NORMAL + RAW
FINE + RAW	FINE
NORMAL + RAW	NORMAL
RAW	FINE

RAW Compression

With the X-H2, you can choose how much to compress a RAW image.

Setting the RAW Compression

1. Go to the menu and choose "I.Q," then select "RAW RECORDING."

2. Choose how you want your RAW images:

   - **[UNCOMPRESSED]:** Larger file sizes because images aren't compressed.

- **[LOSSLESS COMPRESSED]:** Smaller file sizes with reversible compression. Viewable with specific software.

- **[COMPRESSED]:** Smaller file sizes (25-35% less) with non-reversible compression, quality similar to [UNCOMPRESSED].

Image Size

Aspect Ratio

The aspect ratio of an image is a critical factor in defining its visual dimensions, representing the proportional relationship between its width and height. Commonly expressed as a ratio, this characteristic plays a pivotal role in how the visual content is perceived. To delve into specifics, widely used resolutions such as 1920 x 1080 or 1280 x 720 epitomize a cinematic 16:9 aspect ratio, signifying that the image is 16 units wide for every 9 units in height. In contrast, the resolution 640 x 480 adheres to a more square-like 4:3 aspect ratio, indicative of a balance where the width is 4 units for every 3 units of height.

For filmmakers and content creators, the choice of aspect ratio is paramount and should align with the intended viewing platform. Consider a scenario where a filmmaker opts for a 4:3 aspect ratio to evoke a vintage aesthetic, aligning with the dimensions of an older television. Conversely, a widescreen 16:9 aspect ratio would be the preferred choice for content destined for display on modern widescreen devices. This meticulous selection ensures that the visual narrative harmonizes seamlessly with the viewer's experience, avoiding unnecessary cropping or stretching that may compromise the intended cinematic impact.

Picture Size

There are lots of picture sizes. If you have more pixels, your picture has more detail, which also makes the file bigger. You can choose options based on the picture's shape.

Sizes available for a [3:2] aspect ratio

Setting	Image Size
[L]	7728 x 5152 pixels
[M]	5472 x 3648 pixels
[S]	3888 x 2592 pixels
[M] SPORTS FINDER MODE with 1.25X CROP	6000 x 4000 pixels

Sizes available for a [16:9] aspect ratio

Setting	Image Size
[L]	7728 x 4344 pixels
[M]	5472 x 3080 pixels
[S]	3888 x 2184 pixels
[M] SPORTS FINDER MODE with 1.25X CROP	6000 x 3376 pixels

Sizes available for a [1:1] aspect ratio

Setting	Image Size
[L]	5152 x 5152 pixels
[M]	3648 x 3648 pixels
[S]	2592 x 2592 pixels
[M] SPORTS FINDER MODE with 1.25X CROP	4000 x 4000 pixels

Sizes available for a [4:3] aspect ratio

Setting	Image Size
[L]	6864 x 5152 pixels
[M]	4864 x 3648 pixels
[S]	3456 x 2592 pixels
[M] SPORTS FINDER MODE with 1.25X CROP	5328 x 4000 pixels

Sizes available for a [5:4] aspect ratio

Setting	Image Size
[L]	6432 x 5152 pixels
[M]	4560 x 3648 pixels
[S]	3264 x 2592 pixels

[M] SPORTS FINDER MODE with 1.25X CROP	4992 x 4000 pixels

CHAPTER 4: TAKING CHARGE OF EXPOSURE

Introducing the Exposure Trio: Aperture, Shutter Speed, and ISO

Getting the right amount of light is crucial to capturing good photos. When taking a photo, the light goes through the camera lens and can be controlled by the aperture and shutter. Exposure is about getting the perfect amount of light on the camera sensor – not too much (overexposure) or too little (underexposure), but just right, like Goldilocks finding the perfect balance.

Think of aperture, shutter speed, and ISO like a triangle for taking good photos. If you mess with one, you must tweak the others to balance things and get the right picture brightness.

Aperture

Imagine the aperture as the camera's eye. It's in charge of figuring out how much light should come in. We use a special number, the f-number, to show this. When the f-number is small, like f/1, it means the camera's eye is wide open, allowing lots of light to come in. On the other hand, when the f-number is big, like f/16, it means the camera's eye is more closed, letting in less light.

Now, those small f-numbers (with big openings) are what we call "fast." It's like the camera's eye opening wide quickly to let in a bunch of light in a hurry. This is really handy when we want to take pictures fast, especially when things are moving quickly or if it's not too bright outside. However, the big f-numbers (with small openings) take more time to let in light. It's like the camera's eye slowly opening. This can be useful when we want to take our time with pictures or when there's already plenty of light around. So, the aperture, with its f-number, helps the camera decide how fast or slow it should let light in, which is super important for capturing great photos!

Aperture and Light

Think of the camera lens like the eye of a camera. When it's darker and you want more light for your photo, you can open up the lens. We do this by using a smaller f-number. It's like making the hole in the camera lens bigger.

Imagine you're in a room that's not very bright, and you want to take a picture. If you use a small f-number, like f/2, it's as if you're telling the camera to open its eye wide. This allows more light to come in, brightening up your photo. It's kind of like opening the curtains on a cloudy day to let more sunlight into your room.

So, adjusting the lens by lowering the f-number is like giving the camera a way to see better in the dark. It's a cool trick photographers use to capture brighter and clearer photos when the light isn't so strong.

Sunny 16 Rule

Use f/16 when it's sunny for good photo exposure – the sunny 16 rule.

Looney 11 Rule

Also, for taking pictures of the moon, remember to use an aperture setting of f/11, following the Looney 11 rule.

Aperture and Depth of Field

The aperture is really important because it decides how much of the picture looks clear and sharp. When we talk about a bigger aperture, it means making the opening in the lens larger. But here's the cool part: a bigger aperture also makes only a small part of the picture in focus, like the main subject. The rest, both in front and behind the subject, becomes blurry.

Imagine taking a picture of your friend with a big aperture (small f-number like f/2). It's like saying, "Let's focus on just my friend." Everything else, like the background and foreground, becomes kind of dreamy and out of focus.

Now, if you want more things to look clear, like the background or foreground, you use a smaller aperture. This means making the opening in the lens smaller. So, when you use a higher f-number, like f/8 or f/16, it's like telling the camera, "Let's keep lots of things in focus, not just one thing."

In photography, this is a neat trick to decide what part of the picture you want to stand out and what you want to be a bit blurry. So, the aperture is like your tool to make the photo look exactly the way you want it to.

Aperture and Bokeh

When you take a photo and the background looks all blurry, photographers call it "shallow depth of field." It's like saying only a small part of the picture is super clear, and the rest is kind of dreamy.

Now, in Japan, they have a special word for those blurry lights in the background – they call it "bokeh." Imagine you're taking a picture of a friend, and behind them, there are twinkling lights. When you use a big aperture (small f-number), those lights become beautiful bokeh – kind of like magical circles of light.

What's interesting is that the shape of the bokeh circles depends on the lens and aperture you use. Some lenses make round bokeh, while others might make it look like stars or even like little polygons (that's just a fancy word for shapes with many sides, like a stop sign). So, when photographers talk about bokeh, they're talking about those lovely, blurry lights in the background that add a touch of magic to the photo.

Aperture and Sun Stars

Have you ever seen pictures or videos where the sun looks like a twinkling star with rays of light? You can create this cool effect by adjusting your camera's opening. When you make the camera's eye opening smaller (using a higher f-number), it can turn bright spots, like the sun, into beautiful star shapes with rays shooting out.

The number of rays you see depends on something called "lens blades" in your camera. Think of them like the pieces of a pie inside your camera lens. The more blades there are, the more rays you'll see. It's like the blades work together to shape the light and make it look like a sparkling star.

A little reminder: even though this effect is awesome, it's important not to stare directly at the sun, as it can hurt your eyes. Also, try not to keep your camera pointed at the sun for too long, as it could cause damage. So, it's a neat trick to make the sun look extra special, but we need to be careful while doing it!

Shutter speed

In photography, shutter speed is how long the camera stays open. It's like the time the light touches the film or sensor. In videos, it's how long each frame is exposed, usually ranging from a few seconds to a fraction of a second.

How Shutter Speed Affect the Look of Footages

Photography

In photos, things in motion will look blurry if you use a slow shutter speed, but if you use a fast shutter speed, they'll appear sharp and still. For instance, when you see pictures of ocean waves looking smooth, it's probably because the photographer used a slow shutter speed.

Videography

A slower shutter speed makes videos blurry but smoother. A faster shutter speed gives clearer images, but moving objects might look jittery. It applies when you're moving the camera, too.

Keep your video smooth by following this simple rule: set your shutter speed close to double your frame rate. For example, if you're filming at 24 frames per second, aim for a shutter speed of around 1/48. It's called the 180-degree shutter rule. But feel free to break this rule for a specific look—higher shutter for a choppy style, lower for a blurry effect. Remember, stick to one shutter speed for your whole video for a consistent look.

If you're recording videos under fluorescent lights and see flickering or filming a screen and notice scan lines, changing the shutter speed can fix the flicker or lines. Use the camera's flicker reduction feature to sync with the lights and reduce flickering for photos.

Configuring Flicker Reduction

1. Go to the menu, click the camera icon, and select "Flicker Reduction."

2. Choose one of the options:

   - **ALL FRAMES:** Reduces flicker in all images during continuous shooting but may slow down frame rates.

- **FIRST FRAME:** Measures flicker only before the first image in a series and applies the same reduction to all following frames.

- **OFF:** No flicker reduction is applied.

Flickerless S.S Setting

Flickerless S.S. Setting is like a better version of flicker reduction, found in Shutter Priority <S> or Manual <M> mode. It's used for minimizing flicker, especially from high-frequency sources like LEDs. When it's on, you can adjust the shutter speed precisely to match the flicker of lights, like a TV or computer screen, preventing flickering or rolling stripes on the display when the frequencies don't match.

ISO

ISO is like a knob for how much your camera likes light. Turn it down for sunny days (ISO 100), and turn it up for dark places. Lower ISO is less noisy (grainy specks) in your pictures, so keep it low when you can. Test your camera before important shots to find the best ISO.

ISO Sensitivity

ISO determines how well your camera captures light. In low-light situations, use a higher ISO on the Fuji X-H2 (from 64 to 51200) to make the camera more light-sensitive. But be careful; higher ISO can create more noise in photos, so use the lowest ISO possible.

Raise ISO for quicker shutter speeds in low light to prevent blur—lower ISO in bright conditions for wider apertures or slower shutter speeds.

Setting the ISO for Still Images

❖ To adjust the ISO on your camera:

➢ Press the <ISO> button or <MENU>.

➢ Navigate to [camera icon] and then [ISO].

❖ Choose from these options:

➢ [AUTO1], [AUTO2], [AUTO3]: Camera sets ISO automatically.

➢ 125-12800: You pick a specific ISO value.

➢ [L(64)], [L(80)], [L(100)], [H(25600)], [H(51200)]: Use these cautiously as they affect image quality.

Setting the ISO for Movie Recordings

1. Push the <ISO> or <MENU> button, go to [Movie mode], then choose [ISO].

2. Pick:

● **[H(25600)]:** Use only when needed, as it may cause speckles.

● **125-12800:** Choose your ISO value manually.

- **[AUTO]:** Let the camera automatically pick the ISO.

ISO Auto Setting

You can choose from three auto ISO settings: [AUTO1], [AUTO2], and [AUTO3]. Each setting lets you pick a starting sensitivity [DEFAULT SENSITIVITY] and a maximum sensitivity [MAX. SENSITIVITY], and the slowest shutter speed allowed [MIN. SHUTTER SPEED]. When sensitivity is on auto, the camera automatically adjusts ISO between your chosen minimum and maximum values. It only increases sensitivity if necessary to maintain proper exposure when the shutter speed exceeds the minimum set in [MIN. SHUTTER SPEED].

When your camera is in Aperture Priority Mode or Auto mode with ISO set to AUTO, the [MIN. SHUTTER SPEED] setting becomes essential. This setting determines the lowest shutter speed at which the ISO adjusts. For instance, set a fast shutter speed if you're capturing fast-moving scenes and want to avoid blurriness. The camera might lower the shutter speed if it's too dark at the chosen aperture; however, if the speed goes below your [MIN. SHUTTER SPEED] setting, the camera will increase ISO instead of slowing down the shutter speed to ensure proper exposure.

Configure the ISO Auto Options

1. Open the menu, go to ISO, and pick an automatic option ([AUTO1], [AUTO2], or [AUTO3]).

2. Move the focus stick suitable < ► >, then up or down to choose what you want to change ([DEFAULT SENSITIVITY], [MAX. SENSITIVITY], or [MIN. SHUTTER SPEED]).

3. Move the focus stick right < ► >, then up < ▲ > or down < ▼ > to set a value.

For [DEFAULT SENSITIVITY], you can choose from 125 to 12800. [MAX. SENSITIVITY] ranges from 400 to 12800. [MIN. SHUTTER SPEED] can be set between 1/500 to 1/4 Sec or [AUTO] for the camera to automatically select a fast enough speed to avoid blurry photos caused by shake or movement.

CHAPTER 5: CAPTURING VIDEO

Recording Movies

To record a movie, you have a few options. You can use the <P>, <S>, <A>, or <M> modes by setting the mode dial and pressing the movie recording button to start and stop. Alternatively, you can choose the dedicated <> Movie mode, where you control movie recordings with the shutter button. In this mode, you can also fine-tune settings like Program AE, Shutter Priority AE, Aperture Priority AE, or Manual by navigating to <MENU> → [Movie mode]→ [SHOOTING MODE].

When you start recording a movie, you'll see a recording symbol [•] and the time left for recording at the top of the screen. It will also display the time you've already spent recording underneath.

Video Resolution

Video resolution is like the size of a movie, but it's not how much space it takes up in megabytes or gigabytes. Instead, it's about how many pixels make up the picture. The common sizes are 4K (3840 x 2160), Full HD (1920 x 1080), HD (1280 x 720), and Standard Definition (640 x 480). For big HD and 4K TVs, it's best to go for 4K or Full HD resolutions.

If you're unsure what size to use, it's better to pick the highest resolution as long as your memory can handle bigger files. You can make the picture smaller later without losing quality. Choosing a smaller size might harm picture quality when making it larger. Use standard definition for limited memory or faster download times on the Internet.

Resolution numbers tell you how many pixels are on a screen. Pixels are tiny dots that show colors to create a picture. More pixels mean a clearer picture. In a resolution like 1920 x 1080, 1920 is the width, and 1080 is the height. So, there are 1920 pixels from left to right and 1080 pixels up and down, totaling 2,073,600 pixels.

Frame Rate

A video is like a bunch of pictures shown quickly, one after another. Frame rate is how many pictures are taken in one second, also called FPS (frames per second). A higher frame rate means more pictures are taken faster.

Which Frame Rate to Choose?

Movies typically use 24 frames per second (fps) globally, providing a cinematic feel with natural motion. Opting for 24 fps is also advantageous for web use as it downloads faster and requires less storage. Television broadcasts in NTSC regions (like the U.S.) often use 30 fps, while PAL regions (like Europe and parts of Asia) use 25 fps. For broadcast purposes, it's recommended to match these frame rates for a more realistic appearance with less motion blur.

Filmmakers use 60 fps or higher for cool effects like slow motion. They shoot faster (over crank) and then slow down the footage to 24 fps for a nice slow-motion look. At 60 fps, moving things look sharp and vivid, which is excellent for sports or action scenes. The blur in your footage depends on both frame rate and shutter speed settings.

Movie File Format and Compression

The Fujifilm X-H2 lets you pick from 10 different types of movie files and compression options.

H.264 vs H.265

The first part of how movies are saved and made smaller is codecs. A codec is like a computer trick that squeezes video files so they're not too big. But it has to keep the video looking good, too. There are two main choices: H.264, which is older but works everywhere, and H.265, newer and called High-Efficiency Video Coding (HEVC). H.264 is easy to edit and share, while H.265 is newer, making files even smaller, but it can be harder to edit and take more time.

ProRes

The X-H2 has an advantage because it can record in ProRes, a video format made by Apple. While ProRes doesn't make your videos look better, it's easier to work with in video editing programs. If you've experienced issues with videos not playing smoothly during editing, using ProRes reduces the need to convert to another format before editing. However, keep in mind that ProRes files are larger than other options.

The X-H2 camera lets you choose from three types of ProRes recording: ProRes 422 HQ (High Quality), ProRes 422, and ProRes 422 LT (Light). The main difference is how much data they store in each picture. ProRes 422 HQ is for top quality with a data rate of 220 Mbps. ProRes 422 has a slightly lower quality with a data rate of 147 Mbps. Lastly, ProRes 422 LT is more compressed for smaller file sizes, with a data rate of about 102 Mbps. Use ProRes 422 LT when you want to keep your files smaller.

All-I vs LongGOP

Now, let's talk about how the XT-5 compresses videos. It has two types: ALL-Intra (ALL-I) and Long GOP. Long GOP stands for Long Group of Pictures, which focuses on tracking the differences between frames. If you're recording something like a sit-down interview where the background stays mostly the same, Long GOP can help make the video file smaller by only capturing changes in each frame.

All-Intra compression makes videos where each frame is treated as a keyframe, allowing for high-quality and frame-by-frame editing. This method keeps a lot of data, resulting in larger file sizes. It's suitable for videos with many changes between frames, like camera pans or action scenes.

420 vs 422

The 3-digit number is like a code for colors in a video. Y is for brightness, U is for blue, and V is for red. This system, called YUV, uses math to mix brightness and color for the final image.

85

There are two options, 4:2:2 and 4:2:0. 4:2:2 is more accurate with colors but needs more power and makes larger files. 4:2:0 is suitable for most situations without heavy editing.

MOV vs MP4

The end part of a movie file involves something called a container. A movie file isn't just the video; it also has sound, details about the video, and other stuff. All this stuff needs to be kept together, which we call a container. Two examples of containers are MOV and MP4.

Apple made MOV, and it works well on Apple devices like iPhones and Macs. On the other hand, MP4 is more universal and works with lots of different devices and software. If you're making videos for social media, MP4 is great because it keeps good quality, makes small files, and is likely to work on most social media sites. But MOV might be a better choice if you want the absolute best quality, especially on Apple devices.

Bit Depth

Bit depth, or color depth, decides how many colors a camera can capture in a video. The higher the bit depth, the more shades and colors the camera can record. For example, an 8-bit camera can capture 256 levels of each color, allowing for over 16.7 million colors. On the other hand, a 10-bit camera records 1024 color levels, offering a potential for more than a billion different colors, resulting in higher video quality.

Most devices like TVs and phones show videos in 8-bit, and that's generally okay for recording. However, using 10-bit gives you more control and better quality when editing videos later. It's like having more colors to work with, so when you adjust things like brightness or contrast, there's less chance of seeing weird color issues. In simpler terms, it's like editing a detailed photo (10-bit) versus a simpler one (8-bit), where the detailed one holds up better during edits.

Setting the Movie File Type and Compression

Choose your video settings in simple steps:

1. Go to <MENU> and select [Movie Mode].

2. Navigate to [MEDIA REC SETTING] → [File Type and Compression].

3. Pick the option that suits your needs:

   - **[H.264 ALL-I 420 MOV]:** High compression, 8-bit depth, All-I interframe, 4:2:0 chroma.

   - **[H.264 LongGOP 420 MOV]:** High compression, 8-bit depth, Long GOP interframe, 4:2:0 chroma.

   - **[H.264 LongGOP 420 MP4]:** For Internet uploads.

   - **[H.265 ALL-I 420 MOV]:** Higher compression, 10-bit depth, All-I interframe, 4:2:0 chroma.

   - **[H.265 LongGOP 420 MOV]:** Higher compression, 10-bit depth, Long GOP interframe, 4:2:0 chroma.

- **[H.265 ALL-I 422 MOV]:** Higher compression, 10-bit depth, All-I interframe, 4:2:2 chroma.

- **[H.265 LongGOP 422 MOV]:** Higher compression, 10-bit depth, Long GOP interframe, 4:2:2 chroma.

- **[ProRes HQ MOV]:** Records in ProRes 422 HQ format.

- **[ProRes 422 MOV]:** Records in ProRes 422 format.

- **[ProRes LT MOV]:** Records in ProRes 422 LT format.

Proxy recording

Recording high-quality videos, like ProRes format, means bigger file sizes because of all the data. Editing such large files requires a powerful computer. If you don't have one or want a smaller video for social media, you can use proxy recording. It captures a high-quality and smaller version, making it easier for smartphones or web hosting. Fuji X-H2 only supports proxy recording for ProRes videos.

How to Enable/Disable Proxy Recording

- To see the Movie Settings List, go to <MENU>, then choose [Movie Mode], and finally select [MOVIE SETTING LIST].

- If you've set ProRes as the MEDIA REC SETTING, find the "Proxy" option at the bottom left. Choose it and press <MENU/OK>.

- Choose one of the following:

  - **[ON (H.264)]:** Records a simultaneous proxy video in H.264 format.

  - **[ON (ProRes Proxy)]:** Records a simultaneous proxy video in ProRes proxy format.

  - **[OFF]:** Does not record a proxy video.

Bit Rate

Bit rate is how many data bits can be sent in one second. If you have a higher number, the video quality is better. To set it:

1. Go to <MENU> → [Movie Mode] → [MEDIA REC SETTING] → [Bit Rate]

2. Choose a Bit Rate:

   - [50Mbps]

   - [100Mbps]

   - [200Mbps]

   - [360Mbps]

   - [720Mbps]

Data Level Setting

A video signal has color mixed with black-and-white info. Fujifilm has two settings for the black-and-white part: [VIDEO RANGE] and [FULL RANGE]. In [VIDEO RANGE], 8-bit videos have a black-and-white range of 16-235, and 10-bit videos have a range of 64-940. In [FULL RANGE], 8-bit videos have a range of 0-255, and 10-bit videos have a range of 0-1023.

Digital video systems like televisions have specific ways of representing colors. For example, they see black as 16 and white as 235. However, computers use a different scale: black is 0, and white is 255. If a video made for a TV is played on a computer, the computer adjusts the colors, but the quality may need to improve. Similarly, some colors may get lost or look different if a computer video is played on a TV.

If you're uploading a clip without editing brightness, contrast, or color, use 16-235 (VIDEO RANGE). But if you plan to edit and enhance the video, choose 0-255 (FULL RANGE) for a wider range of tones and better editing options.

Setting the Luminance/ Data Level

- Go to the menu, choose "Movie Mode," and select "Data Level Setting."

- Now, pick a data level:

  - For "Video Range," if it's an 8-bit signal, the range is 16-235. For a 10-bit signal, it's 64-940.

- For "Full Range," if it's an 8-bit signal, the range is 0-255. For a 10-bit signal, it's 0-1023.

Movie Audio Settings

Audio Level Display

When making a movie, check your Microphone's audio levels to ensure it captures sound properly. The display shows softness at the bottom and loudness at the top. If there's no sound, no bars light up. Red bars at the top mean it's too loud for a good recording. Aim for sound levels in the middle for the best audio quality.

Audio Rec Level Adjustment

If your sound is too quiet or loud when recording, you can adjust the microphone level. If it's too quiet, turn the level up (to the right), and turn it down if it's too loud.

Setting the Audio Rec Level for the Internal Microphone

1. Go to the menu, choose [Microphone], then select [INTERNAL MIC LEVEL ADJUSTMENT].

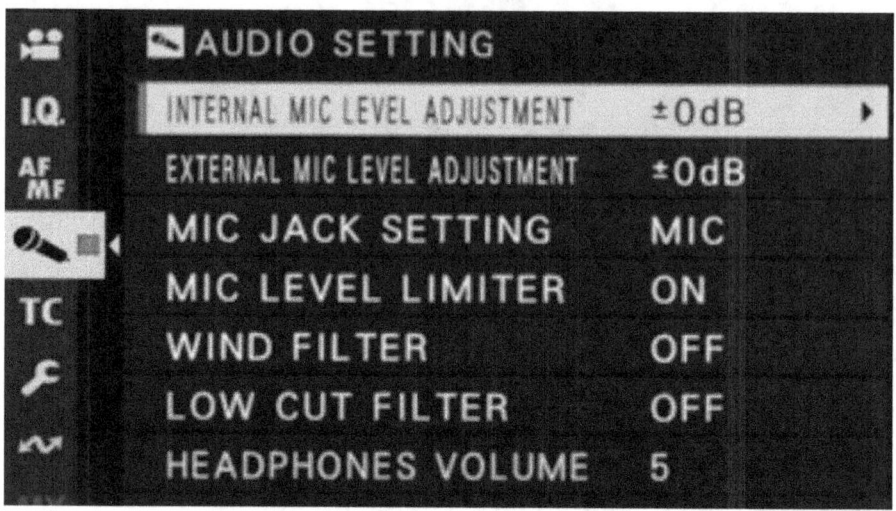

2. You can let the camera automatically set the microphone level with [AUTO] or manually adjust it with [MANUAL]. If you choose [MANUAL], use the focus stick to select from 25 recording levels.

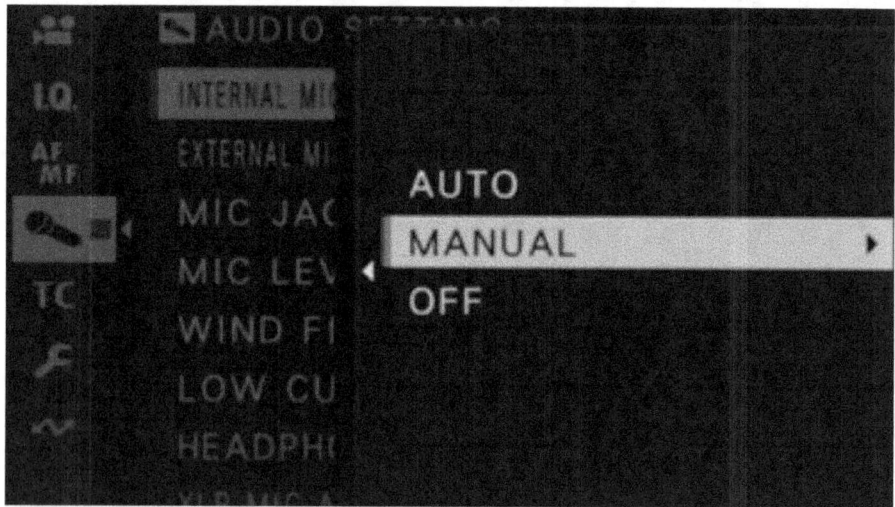

If you want an external microphone, plug it into the 3.5mm jack on the camera's side. Note that microphones needing plug-in power won't work. You can adjust audio levels when using an external microphone, but you'll find that setting in a different menu option.

Setting the Audio Rec Level for an External Microphone

1. Choose from the menu by selecting [Microphone], then navigate to [EXTERNAL MIC LEVEL ADJUSTMENT].

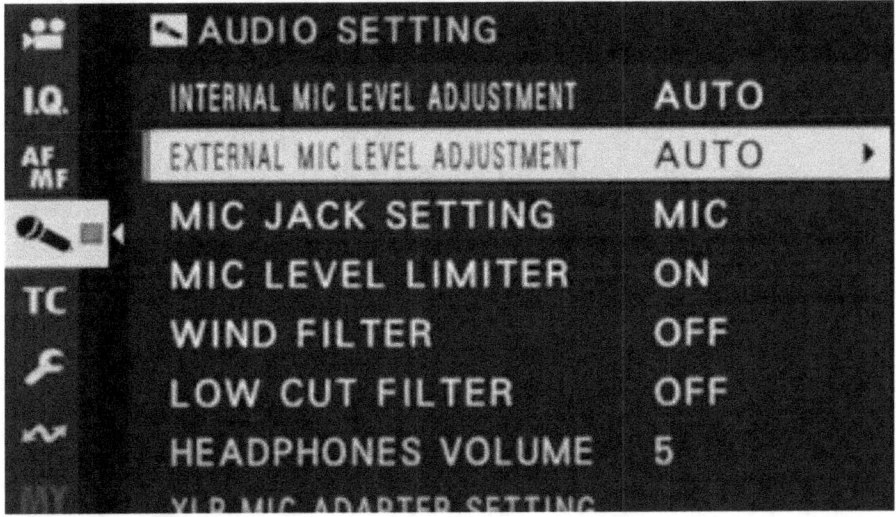

2. Choose:

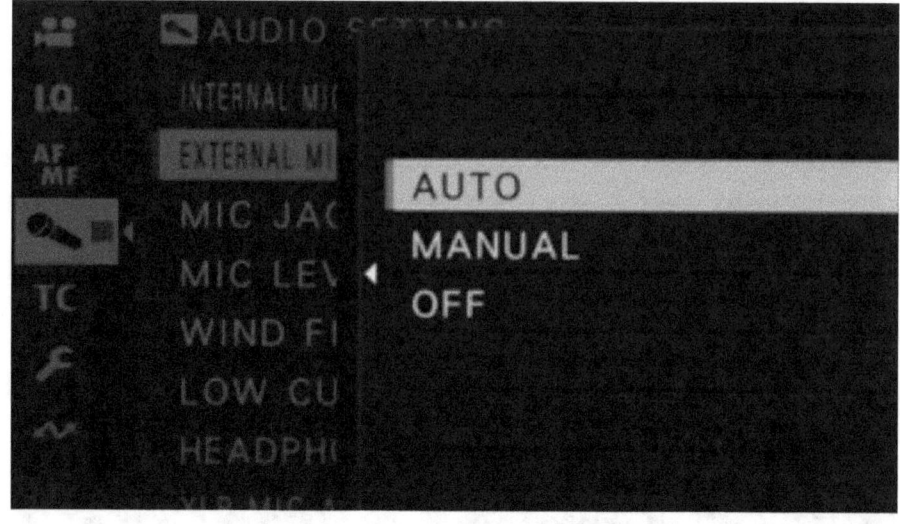

- [AUTO] for automatic external microphone sound level adjustment by the camera.

- [MANUAL] to manually adjust the microphone input level. Tilt the focus stick right to select from 25 recording levels.

- [OFF] to disable the external Microphone and prevent sound recording.

Microphone Level Limiter

Apart from changing how loud the sound is when you record, you should consider turning on the Mic Level Limiter. It helps prevent distortion when the sound is too loud for the Microphone. It's better to have the audio too quiet when recording because you can make it louder later. But if it's too loud and distorted, it's tough to fix.

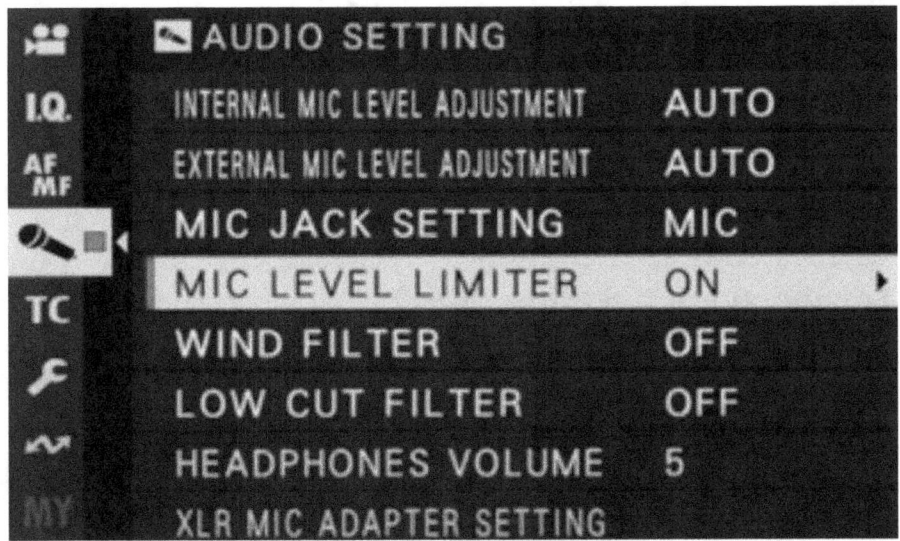

The Microphone Level Limiter on/off

Go to MENU, then choose Microphone, followed by MIC LEVEL LIMITER. You can turn it ON or OFF.

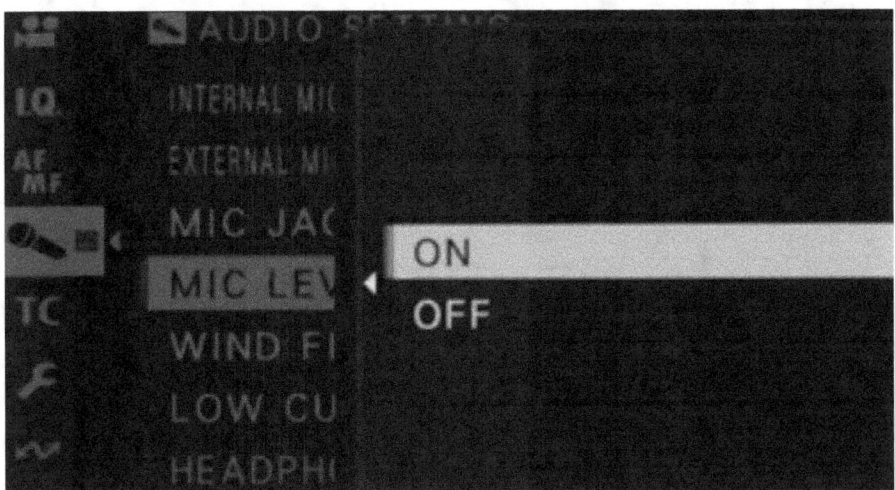

Wind Noise Reduction

When you're recording in windy places, the video might capture the sound of the wind in the camera's Microphone, making it distracting or blocking the intended audio. To fix this, use the Wind Filter with the camera to reduce wind noise.

Turning the Wind Filter on/off

Choose "Microphone" from the menu, then select either "ON" or "OFF" for the "Wind Filter" option.

Low Cut Filter

If you want your audio to sound even better in your videos, there's a nifty tool called the "low-cut filter" that you can use. Imagine it as a special helper that works to reduce unwanted background noises, like the humming sound of a fridge or cars passing by, when you're busy recording.

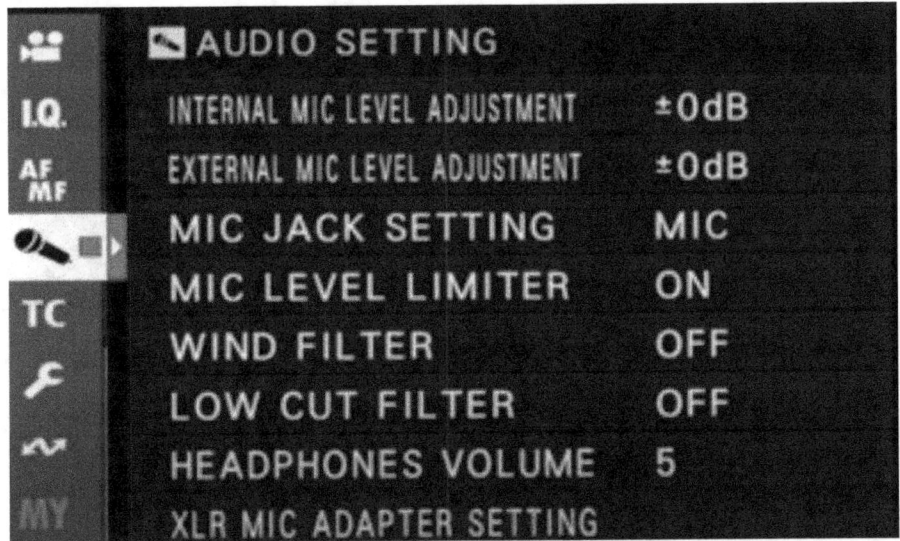

The low-cut filter is like a smart guard for your audio. When you turn it on, it focuses on the lower frequencies, where those background noises often hang out. It kind of says, "Hey, I don't want to hear the low humming or rumbling stuff," and helps to keep your main audio clear and crisp.

Turning the Low Cut Filter on/off

Choose whether to turn the Low Cut Filter on or off by navigating through the menu using the Microphone option.

Headphone Volume

When you connect your headphones to the camera, you open up a world of audio control. It's like having a little sound command center right in your hands. You see, your camera is not just for capturing great visuals; it's also a wizard at managing audio.

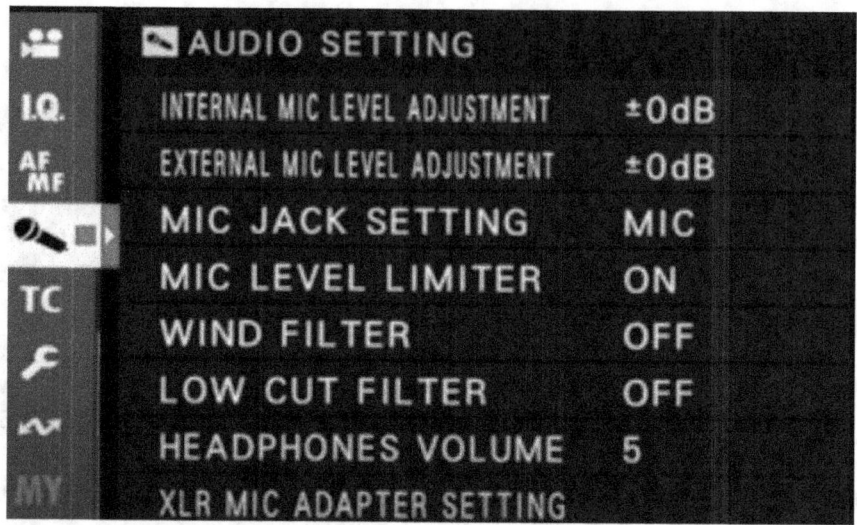

Once your headphones are plugged in, you can tweak and fine-tune the volume to make sure you're hearing everything just right. It's a bit like having your own DJ booth but for the sounds your camera is capturing.

Adjusting Headphone Volume

Choose "Microphone" from the menu, then adjust the volume for your headphones.

Time Code Settings

Timecode is amazing for video makers, especially when you're using different cameras. Imagine you have multiple cameras recording the same event. Timecode is a special code that helps all these cameras play together in perfect harmony.

When all the cameras have the same timecode, it's like they're all following the same clock. This makes life much easier when you're sitting down to edit your video. You can line up the footage from all the cameras so that everything happens at the exact same moment.

Now, the fancy term for timecode that people often use is "SMPTE Time Code." That stands for the Society of Motion Picture and Television Engineers, which is like a group of experts who make sure everything in movies and TV looks just right. The timecode looks like a digital clock with hours (HH), minutes (MM), seconds (SS), and even tiny fractions of a second (oo). The format looks like HH:MM:SS.oo.

Turning the Time Code Display on/off

<MENU> → [TC] → [TIME CODE DISPLAY]→ [ON] or [OFF]

Start Time Setting

You can choose from three ways to set the starting time for the time code display. First, pick [RESET] to begin at oo:oo:oo. Alternatively, use the current time as your starting point. The third option lets you manually choose a starting time code. In the past, cameras were linked to a timecode generator for synchronization. Nowadays, you can achieve the same sync on modern cameras by entering a starting point other than oo:oo:oo:oo in [MANUAL PRESET].

Set the Time Code Start Time

1. Go to the menu, then choose "Start Time Setting."

2. Choose one of the following options:

- Manually set the time code by moving the focus stick to the right.

- Set the time code start time to the current time.

- Reset the time code to 00:00:00:00.

Configuring the Time Code Count Up Setting

1. Go to the menu, choose "TC," and select "COUNT UP SETTING."

2. Choose between:

   - **[Rec Run]:** Time code moves forward only when recording.

   - **[Free Run]:** Time code advances whether the camera is recording. It helps sync multiple cameras during live events, allowing you to match footage from different cameras based on specific time codes.

Drop Frame

When you're busy recording videos at frame rates like 59.94P or 29.97P, there's a neat thing called timecode that you can play around with. It's like a super-organized way of keeping track of time in your videos. Now, here's something interesting – you can set the timecode to work in either drop frame or non-drop frame mode.

The timecode usually follows the beat of 30 frames per second or 60 frames per second, even though the actual frame speed is more like 29.97 or 59.94 frames per second. This tiny difference might not sound like a big deal, but when you're recording for a long time, it can create a little gap between the timecode and real-time.

Here's where drop frame mode comes to the rescue. It's like a smart solution that skips a few frames here and there to make sure the timecode matches up better with the actual time. It's a bit like how we add an extra day to the calendar every four years (leap year) to make up for the tiny bit of extra time in a year.

How to Set Whether to Drop Frames or Not

1. < MENU> → [TC] → [DROP FRAME]

    - Choose "ON" if you want the camera to skip frames to stay in sync with the time code and recording time, shown as 00:00:00.00 (seconds.frames).

    - Choose "OFF" if you want the camera to record the time code without skipping frames, displayed as 00:00:00:00 (seconds:frames).

You can also decide whether the time code is shown on connected HDMI devices.

Tally Light Settings

When you're busy making videos with your camera, there's a little helper called the "tally light." This light is like a tiny signal that tells you the camera is recording all the action. You might find this special light at the back of the camera, the front, or sometimes even in both spots.

Now, here's the fun part – you get to decide how this light behaves. You can choose if it blinks, like a friendly little wink, or if it stays on like a steady guide. It's kind of like giving your camera a little personality.

How to Set the Tally Light

1. Go to the menu, choose "Movie Mode," then select "TALLY LIGHT."

2. Choose one of the following options:

   - The rear indicator lamp stays on steadily while recording.

   - The rear indicator lamp blinks while recording.

   - The front AF assists, and the rear indicator lamps stay on steadily while recording.

   - The front AF assist lamp stays on steadily while recording.

   - The front AF assist lamp and rear indicator lamp blink while recording.

   - The front AF assist lamp blinks while recording.

   - The front AF assist lamp and rear indicator lamp remain off during recording.

CONCLUSION

The Fujifilm X-H2 User Guide has helped you to demystify photography and empower you with the knowledge to unleash the full potential of their X-H2 camera. Armed with an understanding of essential settings, creative techniques, and practical tips, users can embark on a photographic journey filled with endless possibilities.

This guide aimed to bridge the gap between novices and enthusiasts, providing clear and concise instructions while fostering a deeper appreciation for the art of photography. The Fujifilm X-H2, with its advanced features and intuitive design, stands as a powerful tool for capturing moments with precision and creativity.